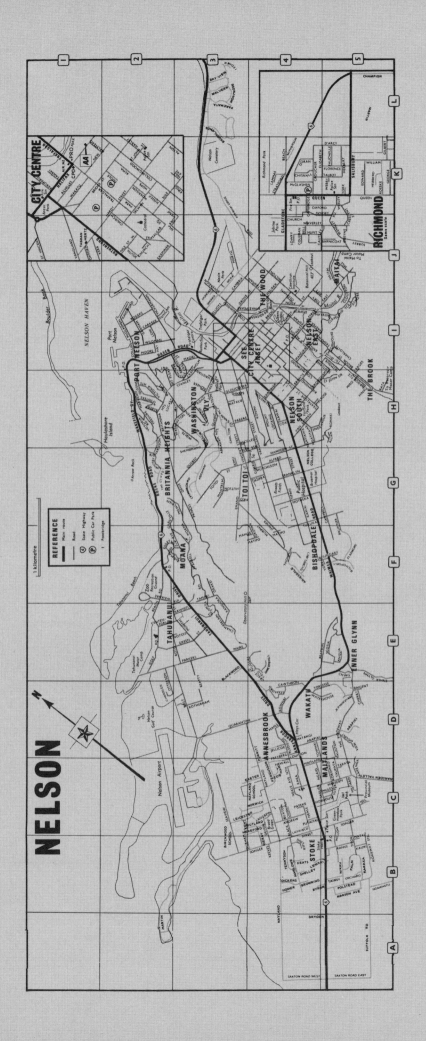

NELSON

Text by **John Acheson** / Photographs by **James Siers**

The Nelson Experience

MILLWOOD PRESS
WELLINGTON, NEW ZEALAND, 1984

ACKNOWLEDGEMENTS

The author would like to thank the following for assistance with the text: Tony Doogue of Nelson/Marlborough National Parks and Reserves Board; Maurice Watson of the Nelson Provincial Museum; John Wheeler of the Nelson Provincial Arts Council; John Savage of the Nelson Historical Society; and Bryce Jones, Nelson Public Librarian. For support and typing, Peter Heath, Yolanda Persico, and Christine Walker of the Nelson Public Relations Office deserve thanks. By way of dedication, so do Jane and our four children for the inspiration of 20 years of shared "Nelson Experience".

First published 1984

MILLWOOD PRESS LTD.
291b Tinakori Road
Wellington
New Zealand

ISBN 0-908582-71-4

Design and production: Publication Graphics Ltd. Auckland
Typesetting: Challis Datacom, Wellington
Printing: Everbest Printing Company, Hong Kong

Contents

INTRODUCTION
An Infinite Variety   5

PART I
Polynesians, Pioneers, and Pip Fruit   7

PART II
Townscapes and Transport Links   18

PART III
Mountains and Marinas   27

PART IV
Trends and Traditions   35

Colour Plates   41

FOREWORD

By His Worship the Mayor, Mr P H Malone OBE

Nelson is a great place in which to live and work and without peer the best place in New Zealand, and perhaps even the world, in which to bring up a family. Nelson City has excellent facilities for education and our region offers unsurpassed recreational opportunities together with a tremendous potential for commercial and industrial developments.

The attractions of our region are diverse and as a first class climate is enjoyed, citizens and visitors alike have every chance to participate in the many recreational activities. The City of Nelson is large enough to be able to provide all of the amenities of civic life without the disadvantages of overcrowding. It is possible to drive six or seven kilometres from a city office to a suburban home for lunch and still return to work within one hour.

As the gateway to a region which boasts two national parks, two forest parks and one maritime park, all within one hour's drive of the City, Nelsonians boast that they have at their doorstep some of the finest mountain, lake and seashore scenery in the world. Nelson is also the sunniest City in New Zealand.

All those who have been involved in the organisation and the production of this publication must be congratulated and to me it is particularly pleasing to hear about the enthusiasm with which this proposal was received and the support that has been given to it by all of the contributing organisations.

On behalf of the citizens of Nelson and the region I extend to all participants our sincere thanks and also the wishes and hopes that the publication will be entirely successful in promoting the benefits of our way of life and standard of living.

Peter H. Malone

INTRODUCTION

An Infinite Variety

Nelson's astonishing variety stems initially from its physical structure—a series of deeply fractured mountain blocks all aligned north-east and south-west, but of very different geological origin. Geologically, from west to east, Nelson contains a virtual cross-section of New Zealand's rock history—from the oldest fossil-bearing formations, found in north-west Nelson, to the youngest of New Zealand's mountain ranges, the Kaikouras.

Where ridges downwarp to sink beneath Cook Strait, a fascinating variety of coastlines is found—giant sandspits, estuaries, boulder banks, shelved and cliffed headlands, drowned valleys, gravel or pakihi terraces. The erosion of these diverse formations has created a connoisseur's choice of beaches around Tasman Bay and Golden Bay.

Lowlands include the fertile Waimea Plains and the lower Motueka Valley, with their close patchwork pattern of crop and stock farming; the dairying valleys of Takaka, Aorere, Murchison, and Rai; and the large central tract of undulating clays and gravels called the Moutere hills, with their multiple cover of pine forest, orchards, pasture and scrub.

Mountain lands include the striking marble formations of the Mount Arthur Range; the unique barren "moonscapes" of the mineral belt east of Nelson city; the remnant of an ancient Gondwanaland continent that forms north-west Nelson; and the sculptured greywacke ridges of the Spenser Mountains.

Whoever arranged the orchestration of the landscapes in the northern South Island did not shrink from challenge, for most elements in New Zealand's landscape are echoed there. The result is neither harsh nor chaotic. All who have seen them would testify to the harmony of such views as the Marlborough Sounds from the air in the early morning; the coves of Abel Tasman National Park from Canaan; the lines of western ridges viewed across a deep Takaka Valley from Takaka Hill; the Heaphy estuary and coastline; the gentle hills on either side of the Rai Valley–Pelorus road; the Waimea Plains against a

shapely Barnicoat Range; and so on. The quintessence of New Zealand's landscapes is to be found within the Nelson region—a microcosm of a country renowned for its amazing landscape contrasts within a small area.

Landscape variety is paralleled by variety of plant cover. Both North and South Island vegetation is seen in the Nelson region. The southern boundaries of the nikau, tawa, hard beech, and silver fern lie in the province. In total about 20 North Island species occur in the Nelson district but not elsewhere in the South Island, and some alpine species reach their northern limits here. Often subtropical species grow alongside stately beech forests more appropriate to a much colder climate. (The kumara in Maori times was never grown very successfully south of Nelson, and today commercial crops such as kiwifruit, tamarillo and avocado would also struggle further south.) As well as northern and southern plant characteristics, Nelson (especially the north-west) has developed a surprisingly large number of endemic species.

Nelson has a riviera climate. Situated in the "sun belt of New Zealand", it is famed for coastal headlands and lofty mountains set against blue sea and sky. Sunshine hours in Tasman Bay and the Wairau Valley are almost always the highest in the country. Rainfall is adequate (1,000 mm for Nelson). The chief beauty of the climate is that the protective arms of the barrier ranges east and west exclude the worst of both Tasman Sea and Pacific Ocean storms.

Edward Jerningham Wakefield in 1842 first pointed out the "very remarkable immunity from wind that causes an almost incredible difference between the climate of Nelson and Wellington, although the two towns are nearly as possible in the same latitude" (just over 41°S). He saw Nelson at its most favourable in a settled month of April (during which he remarked that only three days without sunshine were experienced) for the city does have its windy patches. Nevertheless his was an acute observation of a

5

remarkable weather line between Cook Strait and Nelson. "The wind through Cook Strait seems suddenly to lose its power before reaching the southern part of Blind Bay. Thus it is common for a vessel to be under double-reefed topsails in the Strait, and to have all her sails flapping in a calm sea soon after she has passed D'Urville Is or Massacre Bay."

Protracted bitter southerly weather is almost unknown in Nelson. A cold, wet southerly "buster" can be beating against Kaikoura and Wellington while Nelson city basks in almost windless sunshine. Nelson's rain comes from the north-east when an occasional subtropical depression brings mild, heavy rain for a day or two to swell the Takaka, Motueka, and Pelorus rivers.

The botanical links across Cook Strait have been mentioned; there is also a physical and human closeness. Only 20 km separates the two islands at Cook Strait's narrowest point; latitudes are comparable (Golden Bay lines up with Manawatu for example, and from the bay the highest peak visible is Mount Egmont); and Kapiti Island is an extension of one of the Sound's ridges. The appearance of closeness of the two coasts on a clear day is not entirely an illusion, despite their being separated by one of the world's wild straits.

Nelson people focus on Wellington as much if not more than Christchurch. It is an ambivalence that goes back to the classic Maori period. The earliest Pakeha settlements tried to break the barriers to the south, found only high country sheep trails instead of the promised interior plain, and turned back. The failure of the Nelson railway to link with the rest of the South Island is perhaps symbolic. Nelson's economic, educational, and recreational links more often than not cross the Straits. The camping grounds and recreational areas of the Sounds and Nelson Province are common holiday locations for southern North Islanders. The region, like its sunny bays, tends to look northward.

There is however a tempting parallel between Nelson's human history—as long and distinctive as that of any part of New Zealand—and its botanical evolution. Much comes from the north, much from the south, but there is also a vigorous endemic element. On a framework of happy climate, diverse landscape, and versatile resources, Nelson's inhabitants have stamped their seal of characteristically isolated and distinctive communities. If the South Island seceded—a fanciful but not novel proposition—Nelson would be puzzled at where its allegiance lay. Pushed by a provincial tradition of being wedded to no political party, voting independently at elections and remaining outside the orbit of any metropolis, true Nelsonians could well decide that the assets of their home region were such as to justify taking a path of their own.

There is a "species Nelsoniae" who are recognised by an insistence that the sun belt has everything they require. It is not essential that their great grandparents arrived on one of the first few ships, although this would almost automatically qualify a descendant for that class. True members of the species exude a genteel air of superiority, as if belonging to some rather aristocratic club and unable to imagine why anyone would not wish to be a member. Their independence and parochial pride are as much to do with their assets of climate, landscape, and cultural variety, as with isolation—which is no matter for regret for such hardy specimens. And who can blame them? What matter if the city is a little conservative, and for the pace of big city life one has to go elsewhere?

Such Nelsonians are now an endangered species. The old Nelson image of slow tempo, exclusiveness, polite "cathedral city" tone, and "sleepy hollow" connotations has almost disappeared. So has the air of grievance at being passed by (as it was, of course, by railway and ferry, for example).

The region now burns with new initiatives. A notably cosmopolitan mood is evident among those involved in new industrial and horticultural developments, tourist expansion, retirement interests, or among the young in the van of alternative life-styles. The vigour of the province and its 75,000 people is ensured by the number of vital people who wish to share its advantages—farmers eager to retire there, business people to set up shop, craftspeople to shape their wares, alternative life-stylers to commune, doctors, lawyers, and educationists to practise.

All come to enjoy a favoured natural environment and climate, a rich variety of farmscapes and resources, and a community of diverse life-styles. There are few visitors who remain unimpressed after a stay in Nelson. International travel writer Colin Simpson was certainly not one of them. After five tours of New Zealand, in *Wake up to New Zealand* (1976) he wrote in answer to the question of where he would choose to remain in New Zealand: "I wouldn't be too surprised if I said Nelson."

Multum in parvo—if the province is ever searching for a motto, that Latin tag would perfectly match its qualities. Freely translated, it reads: *just about every advantage confined within a small region.*

PART I

Polynesians, Pioneers, and Pip Fruit

The Cook Strait lowlands of the South Island were a significant region in the culture of New Zealand's first inhabitants, now termed archaic or "moa-hunter" Maori. Most moa-hunter camps were on the grassy, eastern side of the island where a large, flightless bird, the moa, was hunted. It was important as a source of food and clothing, and its bones provided raw material for fish-hooks and artifacts. Much of the knowledge of the relatively peaceful moa-hunters (of whom there is no mention in later Maori tradition) has come from archaeological detection in two areas of Nelson and Marlborough.

The first "dig" to unveil the story of New Zealand's earliest settlers was at the Wairau River bar, in Marlborough. Moa bones and human campsites were discovered there in 1939 by a 13-year-old boy, Jim Eyles, who was to become the first director of the Nelson Museum. A thorough investigation during the 1940s by teams from the Canterbury Museum led by Dr Roger Duff showed the Wairau bar to be a most revealing source of information about pre-classic Maori culture.

Other major evidence has come from a "mineral belt" which runs almost the full length of the Nelson region from D'Urville Island to near St Arnaud. From the pakohe (argillite) they quarried from the hilly fringe of this belt, the early Maori worked flakes into adzes virtually identical with their Polynesian homeland prototypes, but distinct from those made by the later classic Maori. The Polynesian miner humped 60 kilos of rounded granite stones from the boulder bank to be used as hammerstones. These were dropped from a height onto the face of argillite rock to smash away manageable pieces. Large quantities of the flaked rock were then carried back to the coast to be worked and polished at leisure.

Tasman Bay was the mecca for pre-classic Maori seeking pakohe. Rangitoto (D'Urville Island) became the trading centre—the Arahura of the archaic Maori—demanding journeys as difficult as those to the "pounamu" West Coast in later centuries. Argillite quarries established in pre-classic times could have been worked for centuries. The quarry above the Whangamoa River is displayed as a diorama in the Canterbury Museum, and the Rushpool quarry at the head of the Maitai Valley is re-created in the new Maori History Gallery of the Nelson Provincial Museum.

Kumara cultivation developed in the North Island, which became more populous than the South. In classic Maori times (AD 1400–1800) the many coastal indentations from Taitapu (Golden Bay) to Totaranui (Queen Charlotte Sound) were home to successive North Island tribes, pushed inexorably south by population pressure and war. The mild climate, plentiful estuary and sea resources, and sheltered inlets attracted the North Island exiles. Life in the coastal and customarily headland sites of the small pa of pre-European times is well outlined in *The Tatooed Land* by Barry Brailsford: "Mobile hapu units based in a pa stronghold moved out to hunt birds, gathered shellfish from mud flats, trap eels and fish the coastal waters."

Soil and climate were adequate in some spots for the kumara to be grown as an added resource. To create a kumara garden of about 500 hectares the Maori modified soil by adding fine gravel, sand and silt dug from nearby pits. Soil structure was improved by burning heaps of wood over the plots. Today such plots of so-called Maori soils are distinguished by their blackness and warmth. The best example lies near the mouth of the Waimea River. A large labour force must have been required to establish these gardens. Signs of small kumara plantations have been found along the west coast, sometimes on sunny slopes where the soil was good.

By 1800 the Ngati Apa, Rangitane, and Ngati Kuia, together with remnants of their predecessors, Ngati Tumatakokiri, claimed and periodically occupied parts of the Nelson Province. The final invasion from the north before European settlement was that of Te Rauparaha and his Ngati Toa tribe. The inhabitants of coastal pa, from D'Urville to Cape Farewell, were routed by Ngati Toa war parties between 1828 and 1830. From their home pa on Kapiti Island, the Ngati Toa thought nothing of canoeing across Raukawa (Cook Strait) to Grassmere salt marshes for a winter supply of duck, and the prospect of doing battle with the Ngati Tahu, paramount tribe of the South Island, provided an even stronger incentive to make the crossing. There were few districts in the north of the South Island over which the Ngati Toa had not extended their sway by 1840. European settlement in the 1840s took place at a time of tribal disruption, and extreme uncertainty over land ownership.

Despite a golden age of earliest Polynesian settlement, Maori impact is not particularly noticeable on the countryside today. The most significant area of Maori reserve land is that upon which part of Motueka is built. Some Nelson city land is also reserved, and other examples are along stretches of the Golden Bay coast, Delaware Bay, and D'Urville Island. A few Maori families descended from historic tribes live in all these districts. There is an urban marae, Te Awhiri, of 25 years standing at Motueka, which is made good use of by summer seasonal workers of the Maori race. Another urban marae, Whakatu, has recently been founded for Nelson.

In the mists of ancient tribal lore of the Ngati Tumatakokiri was the tale of the arrival of two strange ships, larger but less manageable than Maori canoes. Eileen Duggan, Marlborough born poet, gives a pakeha version of what the arrival of New Zealand's first European visitors might have been like:

Two islands he charted, and—end of a
dream,
See, from the north there near Maria Van
Dieman,
Tasman drew the first chart and for more
than a century,
A line it was, two curves and a headland . . .

The navigator was Dutchman Abel Tasman; his ships were *Heemskerck* (60 tons) and *Zeehaen* (100 tons); the time was December 1642. The two curves in Tasman's map represent Golden Bay (which he had named Murderers' Bay) and Tasman Bay (the "Blind Bay" of Captain Cook). The headland between them is Separation Point. This first European interaction with New Zealand's Polynesian inhabitants was fatal: four crew of one of the Dutchman's longboats were killed after being rammed by a Maori canoe, just off that headland. This historic clash—and the first European sighting of New Zealand—is commemorated by a stark, dignified obelisk dramatically sited on a minor headland between Ligar Bay and Tarakohe.

Tasman sailed away, disheartened by the Maori attack and without trying to land on his newly discovered "Staten Landt". Almost two centuries passed before Europeans were to

appear again in the two bays. Between times, however, Captain James Cook completed his circumnavigation of New Zealand in 1769 by sighting once again the island he had named "Stephens" at the northern tip of D'Urville. He found Ships Cove in Queen Charlotte Sound an ideal anchorage for overhauling his vessels, and it was from here in early 1770 that the first close observations of New Zealand and its Polynesian people were made.

After Cook's voyages of discovery there was another gap until in 1826–7 the Tasman Bay coastline was surveyed by the outstanding French navigator, Dumont D'Urville, whose Gallic placenames are dotted on both sides of the bay—Adele, Astrolabe, Coquille, Pepin, Croisilles, French Pass.

In the early decades of the nineteenth century sealers used this coast. The first of these adventurers of the South Pacific remain anonymous. Closer to the period of European colonisation names such as John Guard of Te Awaiti, James MacLaren of Croisilles, and Captain Frederick Moore of the brigantine *Jewess* became well known. In the 1830s seamen, sealers, and land sharks were often helped by, and sometimes lived as part of, small Maori communities in the Sounds and bays. MacLaren became Nelson's first white settler in 1838 when he was given 150 acres at Croisilles harbour. Some of these men were the first land "buyers", hoping to profit from colonialisation, which they perceived to be just around the corner. A few were in turn made good use of by the New Zealand Company as pilots, guides, and advisers on tribal arrangements around the Cook Strait districts.

Frederick Moore was the central character in the last-minute selection of Nelson Haven as site for the New Zealand Company's second colony— a story with something of a mystery attached to it. Moore, familiar with Blind Bay and Motueka Maori from earlier voyages in the recently wrecked *Jewess*, proposed the district to the Wakefields. They seized upon his suggestion and, obtaining Governor Hobson's reluctant permission to colonise outside the Auckland area, Captain Arthur Wakefield took Moore on as pilot for a reconnaissance with the three expeditionary ships, *Will Watch, Whitby* and *Arrow*, which departed Wellington on 2 October 1841. Moore's enthusiasm for the Motueka district led them first to explore harbour and town sites on the Astrolabe-Kaiteriteri coast. Several weeks of exploring Tasman Bay and the lowlands passed, then finally a *Deal* boat, with Moore in charge, landed by chance on the boulder bank on 20 October 1841. To the amazement of the crew there was exposed, in Moore's words, "a sheet of water considerable in extent, and to all appearances a good harbour". Moore had not heard of the possibilities of this place called "Whakatu", and the mystery, now unlikely ever to be solved, is why Pito, one of the Motueka Maori who had in all other respects been helpful, was so reluctant to show the Haven to the *Deal* crew. After exploring one or two other possibilities, Captain Wakefield determined that "Whakatu" could be "the haven of plenty for many pioneers" as Moore had described it. Soon surveyors and labourers were at work preparing the settlement.

The cradle of South Island settlement

Settlers about to found the first organised colony in the South Island drifted down Blind Bay in late January 1842 on the barque *Fifeshire*. They made Nelson Haven early on 1 February, since then celebrated as Nelson's Anniversary Day. The *Fifeshire* was followed a few days later by the *Mary Ann*, and then *Lord Auckland*. The three immigrant ships carried just over 500 settlers.

The New Zealand Company had been set up as a colonising and profit-making venture by E G Wakefield. Nelson, even though an afterthought, became the most ambitious settlement with 201,000 acres needing to be sold, made up of 1,000 allotments of one town acre, 50 suburban acres, and 150 rural acres. The sale of all allotments would obtain for the Company £300,000, of which £130,000 was to be used to pay the passages of immigrants from the labouring class. In England arrangements made for the new colony were hasty; nowhere near enough allotments were sold, and too few of the moneyed men who had bought them were willing to emigrate. By direction of New Zealand's first Governor, Captain William Hobson, the new colony could be no further south than the Cook Strait area, and even though the Company's surveyor, Frederick Tuckett, advised that Blind Bay possessed only 60,000 acres of the required 210,000 of lowland, of which no more than 4,000 acres was first class soil, Captain Arthur Wakefield, leader of the settlement, felt committed.

Insufficient flat land, inadequate land title and lack of capital were to plague all the New Zealand Company settlements in the Cook Strait area, but Nelson most of all. Lack of good land rapidly sparked exploration west to Golden Bay, south to the Buller River, and east to the Wairau Valley—all districts with some of the desired agricultural potential, but far distant from the township planned for Nelson Haven.

Uncertain land ownership caused innumerable squabbles between Maori and Pakeha on both sides of the Strait. There were skirmishes with the redoubtable Te Rauparaha, whose Ngati Toa had dominated the North Island's Kapiti Coast

and the South Island to almost as far south as Christchurch for a generation. By far the grimmest clash concerned the Wairau Valley. To the delight of the Nelson settlement, surveyors had reported in late 1842 that a further 150,000 acres of good land existed over the ranges on the east coast. When the Ngati Toa pulled up surveyors' pegs, a police party was hastily organised to enforce the highly dubious claim to the lower Wairau. The magistrate and special constables became involved in a shooting affray with Te Rauparaha's party and, in what was then termed the Wairau "massacre", several Ngati Toa were killed and over half the pakeha were shot. Those colonists taken prisoner were clubbed to death. The Wairau incident blighted the development of the one-year-old colony. The settlement felt beheaded—and in some ways it was. Captain Arthur Wakefield was now dead along with several of the colony's other leaders. Over the most accessible additional land resource—the Wairau—Te Rauparaha and his nephew Te Rangihaeata had by Maori custom conclusively confirmed their mana.

The next two years were trying ones. The colony experienced not only the post-Wairau panic, but also the drying up of Company funds. The foolhardiness of sending immigrant ships to an unknown territory was compounded by the allocation of land by lottery in a settlement where good land was minimal and there were too many absentee landlords. The middle section of the lowlands at the head of the bay was a disappointment. In the words of the Nelson resident agent of the Company, "nearly the whole of the Moutere district comprising about 200 sections consists of a soil which appears to be deficient in the fundamental compounds of vegetable matter ... indurated gravel almost unmixed with soil". So much for the extensive Moutere gravels—the heart of the Tasman Bay lowlands—until the twentieth century discovered that pine trees would grow exceedingly well on them. The resident agent of 1845 went on to say "portions of all the districts [surveyed], except perhaps Waimea West, extended up the sides and even to the tops of steep hills which can never be ploughed ...".

"Blind Bay" must have seemed an appropriate name to many a struggling settler in the 1840s. No less a surveyor–settler than J W Barnicoat was soon describing the Company practices as "a cruel system of swindling". Both remaining capitalists and hungry labourers in this new Utopia soon realised they would have to get on with their own pioneering.

Sarah Higgins wrote with eloquent simplicity of the time just after the Wairau disaster. As a 15-year-old girl, she had arrived in 1842 with her working-class parents on the *Bolton*. Her first experience in Nelson had been sleeping in a flax hut and listening to her father and brothers taking turns beating the rats off. Then in 1843 "our troubles began. There was no food, no money, no shops. We had to get a few roots and berries, sour thistle and docks, and boil them. We used to get a few fusty and mouldy biscuits . . . and the Maori did bring us some little baskets of potatoes, sometimes for one shilling we would get them . . . but the moneyed men were all gone."

At last the labourers were allowed to take up land themselves and pioneering then became all-absorbing. Sarah Higgins commented: "They were glad enough to get into the country. Men with their families tramped through swamps and rivers carrying their babies, their food and their bedding on their backs for 15–21 miles in the dense bush of Spring Grove to Spooners Range . . . they lived there a number of years, sawing timber and splitting shingles to roof the cottages that were being build on the small sections of 5–10 acres."

Despite the misleading propaganda, the indecent haste to establish a settlement, and the profit motive paramount in England, it is hard to deny some achievement to the New Zealand Company. Without the energy and, in some ways, idealism of the Wakefields most of the 4,000 Nelson settlers of the 1840s would not have got to New Zealand—and the quality of both capitalist and labourer was probably improved by the degree of selection that prevailed. Nelson benefited from the idealism, if not for long from the capital resources, of the Company.

Nor did the Wakefield theory of a high price for land mould the settlement for long. The small number of landlords was to catapult many of the labouring immigrants into the status of small landowners. The unavailability of the wide open spaces of the Wairau for a few years gave Nelson time to develop a social pattern which not only differed from Wakefield's grand design but also—in the absence of the squatters of Canterbury and Otago—anticipated the New Zealand of the small freeholder in the close rural communities of the Waimea Plains which remain to this day.

A social melting pot was at work. An official Anglicanism prevailed, with a bishop installed and a Church of England in almost every settlement. Non-conformist groups were very strong, however, and especially influenced the founding of schools without specific religious doctrine. There was a notable Roman Catholic element. German immigrants soon added to the "pot" by arriving during the middle of the "troubles" of the 1840s. They came from Hamburg in two shiploads. At first allocated the dismaying Moutere district, they soon moved to the more fertile Ranzau and Upper Moutere. Within a few years the German settlements were accepted into the community, contributing their own flavour to it with such additions as the first grapes and hops.

In this society Polynesian still rubbed shoulders with Pakeha in exploration, shipping, and clearing the land, for race relations remained good despite some ripples after the Wairau deaths. The Church of England had to come to terms with dissenters, German and English settlers lived side by side, and labourers became as significant as landlords. A protest by Company labourers to Captain Wakefield in January 1843 (as well as a demand for wages they could live on), included some quite radical arguments. The circumstance was a colony where only one-twelfth of the allocated lots were actually settled by purchasers who according to a working class petition, "on beholding this land and knowing that it wants a deal of work to cultivate it, and they have not got it, are obliged to turn to their original trade of shop keeping etc and thus no export is raised in the colony . . . Now Captain Wakefield, if you do not stretch forth your hand to the working class at Nelson you will never have a colony . . . in fact there is little or no money in the Colony except the Company's . . . we are the only circulating medium."

Though at first refused, the petitioners soon gained their objective—both in better wages, and in the offer of land. This working class analysis of the situation reflected the realities of the new colony. A democratic and independent tone was established from the start, soon to be reinforced by the levelling tendencies of the gold rushes.

Pastoralists and prospectors

Having survived the traumatic 1840s and shaken off links with the New Zealand Company, the embryo colony needed a profitable export. The Nelson Province (which included Marlborough until 1859) played out the overtures to both the gold rush decade and the age of tussock pastoralism in the South Island.

For a short time wool was king. The prototype for large scale sheep runs was established at Flaxbourne in the sweet grassy downs overlooking Cook Strait in eastern Marlborough. In 1847 Weld and Clifford stocked the downs with several thousand merino sheep from Australia, and in the same year crown purchase of the Wairau district from the Ngati Toa secured their possession. Nelson colonists such as Redwood, Fearn, and Richmond took up runs in the Awatere and Wairau working back through Tophouse into the tussock valley of the upper Buller. Once established, these pastoralists did create the capitalist class that the New Zealand Company had failed to attract in sufficient numbers, but the Nelson Province of today is little shaped by the sheep industry or squatter society. Stream and ridge names in tussock

An early view of Trafalgar Street, (Nelson Provincial Museum, Tyree collection.)

basins or tableland tops derived from early runholders or musterers are the chief witness to the pastoral age.

The impact of the gold rushes was more lasting. The province simply contained better mineral prospects than it did sheep country. Gold had been picked up by a Golden Bay settler as early as 1842, and surveyors had noted its presence at other times—but no one seemed interested! Then two musterers, Ellis and James, carried gold back to Nelson to be tested by George Lightband, a prospector with Australian experience, who then proved the worth of the claim at "Lightband Gully". (A memorial cairn to the discovery stands beside the main highway just south of Collingwood.) By early 1857 diggers were arriving by the boatload, and there were soon over 2,000 working the field to create New Zealand's first gold rush. Many of the diggers were out of Californian and Australian goldfields. Tough individualists, they dammed streams, contoured water races around ridges, and panned and sluiced the alluvial drifts on the broad high pakihi terraces cleft by deep gorges to the south of the Aorere River. Gibbstown (as Collingwood was first called) became port of entry and hub of the goldfield. It had its moment of glory as the first boom town of the New Zealand colonies during 1857–8.

Prospecting fever cooled for a few years, but by 1864 every colonial Tom, Dick and Harry seemed to be out looking for the precious metal. The Wangapeka diggings on the eastern slopes of the Tasman Mountains, the Wakamarina rush to a tributary of the Pelorus River, and several fields in the upper Buller valley added colour and wealth to the 1860s. The Port of Nelson took big strides as a supplier to the "Nelson South West Goldfield" through its ports of Greymouth and Westport. Gold was the lure that completed inland exploration in mountainous areas. Gold trails such as the Maungatapu between Nelson and Havelock, and those of the Buller, linked Nelson to the goldfields.

Charles Thatcher, famous balladeer of the 1860s music halls, sang of a favourite method of obtaining gold in one field:

> On the banks of the Wakamarina,
> From Nelson some 32 miles,
> A splendid goldfield's been discovered
> Where dozens are making their piles.
> They dig on the banks of the river,
> And in many a crevice I'm told,
> With your knife you can dig out the
> nuggets—
> A nice easy way to get gold.

The Wakamarina deserved a song. Discovered in 1863 in answer to the Marlborough superintendent's offer of £1,375 for the discovery of a goldfield worth 10,000 ounces, the Wakamarina was one of New Zealand's richest valleys. Several thousand Otago miners decamped for the north, and a thousand arrived in one day at the new diggings. In a few short months the field was extraordinarily rich, very overcrowded, and quite violent—and then the easy gold was gone.

Other rushes occurred later in the nineteenth century, and there was a return to the goldfields during the depression years of the 1930s, but

11

Goldfield engineering on the Wakamarina c.1895 (Nelson Provincial Museum, Tyree collection.)

these episodes cannot compete in their power of legend. Most valleys of the Richmond Range were worked for both alluvial and quartz gold; the Mount Arthur tableland and valleys leading into the Karamea River produced worthwhile gold. The Taitapu estate, south of Westhaven Inlet, gave rich returns over a long period.

Overall Nelson gold earned millions for the province in the nineteenth century. Little remains of the old goldfields. Some trails have been kept up; a mineshaft, an overgrown sluicing tailing, or some rusty equipment can still be sighted. A common experience of early Nelson history whether of the Polynesian past, of early explorers, sealers, whalers, pastoralists or prospectors is that the key to historical imagination is often to be found in out-of-the-way places.

Today searching for the precious metal is merely a prospector's hobby or visitor's relaxation—and there are few Nelson rivers that show no colour. Although according to some definitions Nelson is the most mineral-rich region in New Zealand, mining projects other than for gold have consistently met with frustration. The early collapse of the Dun Mountain copper and chrome venture in 1862–72 was an early example. Problems of mineral exploration in a region of difficult mountain terrain and excessively fractured geology have been considerable. Golden Bay—a place of mining dreams—had hopes of a steel industry with its deposits of coal and Onekaka iron ore. Asbestos mining in the upper Takaka Valley, scheelite in the Richmond Range; uranium above the Buller gorge—all have ephemerally glittered. The steady resources are dolomite, serpentine, and lime for agricultural fertiliser or industrial purposes; Takaka marble and Tarakohe cement for construction. Mineral exploration is still extensive in the mountain lands, and offshore from the Golden Bay for oil. Nelson as well as overseas companies are involved in heavy prospecting investment, and optimism prevails, as always, that an "El Dorado" will one day be found to justify all the effort.

Most pioneering between the gold rushes and World War 1 took place in the block of the Moutere gravels, in the foothills of the high ranges, and in the heavily forested outer valleys. Symbols of these settlements were hill slopes covered in charred tree trunks and valley paddocks of stumps. The smell of smoke hung over the battle between man and forest, as settlers struggled to establish stock of some kind. Not much hill country accepted burning and English pasture before the days of extensive use of artificial fertiliser, and total farm acreage steadily dropped for the next half century as hill land reverted to scrub, gorse, or second growth. Dairying, however, prevailed on the rich, heavy soils of the Takaka, Murchison, and Rai valleys, and at Karamea. Dairy factories were built in the early twentieth century. Pioneering was a battle not only against the land, but also against intermittent agricultural depression. Life for the generally large families tended to be as described by Jessie in *Speaking a Silence*, Christine Hunt's collection of reminiscences of Golden Bay old identities.

"I had to walk three miles to school. Then afterwards there would be more chores at home; getting everything ready for milking, the buckets and that, bringing the cows up through the mud and waterholes and the blackberries as high as the side of a house here, and dodging between the stinging nettles and supplejack vines. Then there would be the milking and separating and butter making, the same old chores—I'd be that tired at night I'd go to bed and never move all night."

Chapel, colonial façade, park and jetty

For the visitor there are some very characteristic, tangible reminders of pioneer days, and it is worth highlighting a few. Indelibly imprinted on the character of Nelson are the many small essays in colonial wooden Gothic architecture, built as labours of religious love, which adorn favoured sites in the province. Pre-eminent in age among small churches is St Johns, sited on the rise behind Wakefield. It is the oldest church in the South Island (built 1846) and second oldest in New Zealand. There is a lovely cluster of churches round the Waimeas, including the impeccably sited Holy Trinity Church, Richmond; St Michaels at Waimea West; and St Pauls, Brightwater. Bishopdale Chapel, next to the bishop's residence in Nelson, has rare distinction. On a hilltop near Ngatimoti a tiny isolated chapel, fine enough sight in itself, is set against the magnificent backdrop of the Mount Arthur marble range. In the far west at Collingwood is small St Cuthberts, designed by surveyor–explorer Thomas Brunner, and in the east at Gentle Annie is an appealing eccentric—a church with a chimney where the cross might be expected, a fireplace being considered necessary to keep itinerant vicars warm for the night! A truly colonial atmosphere can be sensed in the interior or adjacent churchyard of any one of these small masterpieces.

There are a large number of other buildings which retain their nineteenth century appearance—farm and station homesteads with colonial design features of high gables, decorative wooden lattice work, long verandahs and dormer windows. At Waimea West "The Gables", built as a home for the Palmer family in the 1860s and still owned by them, shows off these features perfectly. A few cob buildings (made of packed earth mixed with straw) have lasted, most of them small as the use of cob was an indication of lack of capital in Nelson's early decades. The best preserved and most impressive of the cob homes is Broadgreen, now a historic building open to the public at Stoke. It was built in the 1850s for Edmund Buxton, one of Nelson's wealthier merchants.

An interesting sequence of old façades still prevails in the main street of most rural towns. There is a strong historical presence in the commercial area of Takaka, Murchison, Motueka, Havelock, and Reefton. (Collingwood has been twice razed by fire, the last occasion in 1904.) Nelson quite possibly has more vintage frontages in its commercial centre than any comparable city—though, as earthquake risks, most of these might soon suffer the same demolition fate as Wellington's old city buildings.

With few exceptions, provincial towns are now sufficiently interested in their heritage to

Trafalgar Street c.1910 (Nelson Provincial Museum, Jones collection.)

establish small museums—Takaka, Collingwood, Murchison, and Havelock are examples. Nelson itself has a fully fledged provincial museum, established in a modern building with a recently added wing for Maori displays. It is located at Stoke next to Isel House, the fine old family home of Thomas Marsden, one of the largest landowners of his day in the province. House and museum are set in a glorious parkland of exotic trees, many a century or more old, established from specimens obtained from all over the world. Planting started in the 1850s, and some of the trees—Corsican pine, Sitka spruce, sequoia—are huge specimens of their kind. The trees are underlain by rhododendrons and azaleas, which produce a famous display in late spring. At the entrance to Isel Park is St Barnabas Church, the first stone church erected in the Nelson Province and another durable relic (it has recently been enlarged) of the first period of settlement.

To digress further, exotic trees became a striking feature of Nelson's town and country landscape. Neither the Waimea Plains nor the Moutere hills were heavily forested, so trees could be freely planted. Poplar and willow lined streams, hawthorn and macrocarpa provided shelter belts, while the great bluegums of the Richmond area, the oaks of Clifton and the planes Totaranui brought a little of Europe, North America, and Australia. The exotic stands add to the harmonies of Nelson's landscape, complementing rather than detracting from the remnants of lowland native bush to be found at well-known picnic spots such as Fearon's and Max's Bush, the Murchison domain and Pelorus Bridge.

One of the Wakefield family who visited Nelson in 1889 observed "the chief glory of Nelson is its gardens and plantations . . . there is no spot out of England where English trees and English birds have so completely domiciled themselves as at Nelson". There could be other towns ready to dispute this judgement, but it is noteworthy that the Popes in their reliable *Mobil Travel Guide to the South Island* label Nelson as the "city of gardens and gorgeous sunsets".

Queen's Gardens, the Botanical Reserve, Fairfield Park and the grounds of Bishopdale (all in Nelson), display a fine variety of long established trees; lifetime gardener Jean Lawrence wrote in her *Gardening Tales*: "The gardens surrounding Nelson Cathedral are among the loveliest I know: not prim and mathematically exact, but with a charming mingling of flowers and shrubs, backed by magnificent old trees."

Wharves and jetties are another distinctive feature of the Nelson Province. Before the days of motorised public transport there were no fewer than 14 ports in Golden Bay and the Marlborough Sounds, quite apart from Nelson and Picton. Tedious inland communications demanded sea outlets, and for much of the nineteenth century small cutters and schooners—commonly termed the "Blind Bay hookers" and often locally built—were the answers.

Old wharves, reminders of some specific mineral boom or other regrettably brief local development, can be found at the end of many a quiet road. Examples are West Whanganui, Puponga and Ferntown (coal), Collingwood (gold), Onekaka (iron), Torrent Bay (timber and marble), Riwaka, Mapua, Okiwi Bay, Havelock—along with innumerable more or less private jetties throughout the Sounds. Some of the old timber pile wharves now merely provide a picturesque focal point to a coastal scene, as at Puponga and Onekaka, but in holiday districts such as Waitapu, French Pass, and Havelock, the jetties preserve a more than useful role as access for pleasure boats and small fishing craft. The marine heritage remains, even though coastal trade has ceased.

The garden develops

"The hitherto quite neglected solitude begins to be inhabited, not by huntsmen and combatants, but by men who build huts, and begin to turn the wilderness into garden." Thus in 1843 wrote Lutheran Pastor J F H Wohlers at Moutere, as he reflected on the pleasure of sitting at his fire in his "rough and unpolished house" after a hard day's work. Perhaps he was looking into a crystal ball as he meditated on the destiny of the settlement, for the choice of phrase was apt.

Orchards of pip and stone fruit had done well in the nineteenth century, but the coming of refrigeration meant an export trade was possible. In 1911 a trial shipment of fruit from Nelson under cool storage succeeded on the London market. Suddenly this was the answer to the region's prosperity, and 7,000 acres were planted in a pip fruit "rush" between 1911–16. A report in 1911 questioned the astounding number of apple trees planted in the Nelson and Motueka districts during that year: "This phenomenal rush to the Moutere Bluffs is accounting for most of the importations. Some have gone inland—planting 100 acre blocks 16 or 20 miles from the nearest port and quite out of touch with the railway. Where will this obsession end?" Many failed—the chosen northern Moutere ridges were steeper than any other orchard country in New Zealand, and orchards took seven to eight years to become established. The area in apple and pear trees has since stabilised at between 3,000 and 4,000 acres, and this was responsible for the lion's share of Nelson's wealth for the next half century. An orchard belt was created on the seaward slope of the Moutere hills, dipping to Tasman Bay in a sweep from Mapua to Motueka. The DSIR Appleby Research Orchard and Nelson's privately endowed Cawthron Institute, whose part in establishing techniques for profitable use of very difficult soils would be hard to overestimate, provided scientific back up. Cool storage facilities and an Apple and Pear Marketing Board enabled crates of apples and pears to fill the holds of overseas ships, while irrigation overcame summer droughts.

Currently the Tasman apple belt produces about 40 percent of New Zealand's annual crop, more than half of which is exported. Well over 2 million cartons are exported yearly, making Nelson one of the world's top pip fruit suppliers. In 1962 an apple cannery at Stoke began to process second-grade fruit, and it has since diversified into large-scale fruit juice manufacture. The area in orcharding is not growing significantly, but new planting can be up to 80 trees per hectare, which is double the traditional density.

Tobacco and hops became specialities of the Motueka and Riwaka districts between the wars. All the country's hop requirements are supplied by Nelson—about half the crop—the other half is exported to West Germany. Some hop gardens have been established on the same plot for generations. The major part of New Zealand's tobacco needs is also met by Motueka

Valley tobacco, but production is declining in the face of an uncertain future for that industry.

Raspberry and boysenberry production are well established further inland. Market gardening is productive close to Nelson and Motueka, and some vegetables are grown for processing. Glasshouse production of tomatoes has long been a special feature of the Nelson urban landscape in the Wood area. Grapes are traditional in Nelson, and recently a handful of small scale vintners commenced wine production in a climate of rapid growth for the New Zealand wine industry.

The success of the "garden" was demonstrated when the National Resources Survey concluded in the 1960s that the "area of the Tasman Bay lowlands under 'special crops' in value of output per acre and variety of crop/livestock production was probably unequalled elsewhere in New Zealand". The search for new special crop varieties continues; it is an advantage that many crops are readily interchangeable. Berries galore—gooseberries, blackberries, blueberries, strawberries; rock melons, persimmons, avocado, tamarillos (in milder Golden Bay for the latter two); garlic or solanum as alternatives for tobacco; feijoas—all are possibilities. Although warnings similar to

Transport for Tasman Bay from Port Nelson c.1895 (Nelson Provincial Museum, Tyree collection.)

those sounded earlier about marketing the orcharding rush are heard, the safest bet is thought to be kiwifruit. Fields of the "green gold" are being confidently established in all existing horticultural areas, as well as in Golden Bay and Karamea. Nelson kiwifruit is equal in quality to that grown in Te Puke.

Packing and marketing of new crops has benefited enormously from sophisticated co-operative packhouse facilities developed mainly through the Nelson firm of TNL (Transport (Nelson) Ltd) which also provides an excellent transport system. TNL has developed experimental horticultural programmes such as the 100 acre kiwifruit farm at Karamea and nurseries for crop supply, as well as encouraging individual farmers to try new crops. The packhouse co-operative which started in 1972 with apples only involved over 1,000 growers, and a peak employment of about 1,200 between 1978–80. It now handles every kind of crop—including mussels, known as "KiwiClams".

There has been some growth in stock farming. Dairy production maintains factories at Takaka and Brightwater. In the past two decades the gravel soils and gorse of the Moutere have been won to production in some areas. The Lands and Survey Department and TNL have both established model farms. The use of heavy machinery to break up the land coupled with heavy topdressing of fertiliser has seen first-class sheep and cattle pasture emerge from scrub. Chicken farming is important near Richmond. Deer farming has already changed the face of some properties—high fences for red deer holding paddocks near towns, and deer farms further out are no longer novel sights. Goat farming is being tried on high country land, and there is no lack of pioneering opportunities in stock farming.

But when all is said and done, it is the locally termed "special crops", intensively produced on the small area of good agricultural land (16 percent), which still identify the region. Characteristic sights are apple orchards sloping to the sun and the sea; a Bavarian look about the hopfields and vineyards of Upper Moutere; drying kilns and oasthouses; the summer influx of seasonal workers; packing sheds and workers' baches; the "help yourself" roadside stalls and "pick your own" fields of strawberries and peas; market gardens and plant nurseries; and jet irrigation spraying the crop horizons as the nozzles lazily swivel in the dry spells.

The horticultural significance of the heart of the province is not likely to diminish, but old patterns are changing rapidly and a very large investment is going into horticultural expansion. Kiwifruit has the potential to become a major income earner. Cool storage space for the crop in Motueka is doubling every few years. Fruit juices and fruit processing are winning new

markets; the appearance of the landscape is strikingly altered in some orchard areas by the training of apple trees espalier-style, or the sudden transition from fields to kiwifruit post and wire. And a social change is occurring which accepts the use of small acreage by people who want to test a wide range of crops without necessarily expecting to make a large income from them.

Full circle—forest and sea

Farming staples of the twentieth century—horticulture and stock—are now being challenged by the fresh application of two old resources.

All of the mountain areas—the Richmond and western ranges, and the ridges of the Sounds, as well as the Takaka, Motueka, and Buller valleys—were bush clad originally, and milling of native timbers took place from whaling days. The need for farmland brought virtual destruction of all the lowland and much of the hill country native forest with the all-embracing "burn off". Milling for the first hundred years of settlement was selective and wasteful. Like mines, mills were often tucked away in isolated places with long distance transport problems.

Native forest is now hardly milled at all: the suitability of the deficient gravel/clay soils of the Moutere ridges for the growth of radiata pine has been the key to recent progress, though Douglas fir and one or two other species have also been established. The Moutere ridges were easy to clear and to plant out; road construction was relatively simple; and in 25–30 years the pines reach millable size.

An immigrant doctor from the Shetland Islands had shown what could be done shortly after World War 1. Leaving his treeless home islands, Dr J P (Jamie) Jamieson came to New Zealand and set up in medical practice in Nelson. He deplored what he termed the rape of the New Zealand forests. From 1915 onwards he tested *Pinus radiata* on several hundred acres of the Braeburn property in the Moutere hills. With loving care Dr Jamieson tended his trees. His plantation became a model of what could be done; a mecca for professional foresters as the trees grew towards maturity; and even a source of seed for export, back to the home of the pine in California.

The advantages of the Moutere gravels have helped to create the second largest plantation forest in New Zealand, clothing the ridges between the two forestry villages of Golden Downs and Tapawera. Much of this forest was planted by workers on employment relief schemes during the depression of the 1930s. Recent plantings have been on the foothills that encircle the block of the Richmond Ranges and fringe the eastern Tasman Mountains; on the Buller–Inangahua terraces; and on the western ridges of the Sounds. Many of these plantings are nearing maturity, and will soon provide a massive resource to be tapped. Until a few years ago, exotic forestry was noticeable only on a drive through Golden Downs or the Rai. It is now difficult to turn off the main highway anywhere without coming face to face with hillsides of young pines, a network of forestry roads, or a log truck thundering around a blind corner. Most development is state initiated and owned; but significant plantings are owned by farmers, the Waimea County Council, and the Nelson timber firm of Baigents.

Extensive use of wood preservation has in 20 years turned radiata into the wonder timber of New Zealand construction—for housing, poles, and fence posts. Nelson pioneered the export of wood chips from New Zealand in 1969 when trade was established with Japan. It is still the leading outlet for chips, processed at the Richmond chip mill.

Forest production should be sufficient by the late eighties to justify a pulp mill. Baigents, a large Nelson family firm involved with timber milling since the 1980s, recently came close to establishing a pulp mill at Eves Valley in conjunction with an Australian industrial giant. The proposal is stymied at present by a combination of practical and financial difficulties, and ecological opposition to siting a giant industry in such a pleasant rural zone. In the meantime Baigents are planning a very large timber and chip complex in their Eves Valley site.

The Forest Service has taken some of the sting out of its wholesale adaptation of the Nelson landscape by providing "amenity zones" along highways and around rest areas. The larch forest on the descent from Spooners Range is a beautiful sight in its autumn colour, and an attractive picnicking zone has been established on the climb to the Hope Saddle. In 1953 Coronation Forest of 140 ha was set aside in Spooners for planting by classes of primary school children. This was such a success that an adjacent area has since been allocated for the same purpose.

The healthy rate of plantings in the 1960s, the development of wood preservation since, the growth of chip and log exports to Japan and Australia have really brought the timber industry on stream in Nelson. Forestry production should double during the 1990s, and quadruple in the following generation. It is difficult to see any other form of production beating it for top place in the province.

A maritime tradition has always been present in Nelson, but again it was refrigeration and canning techniques that set up an export trade. Events since 1970 have rapidly outmoded the simple dredging for the shellfish delicacy scallop and the inshore fishing catch of small local boats. Filleting, processing, and freezer facilities of the fish factories, of Skeggs and Sealords, as well as big sea trawlers came on the scene. Japan and other Pacific nations entered joint fishing ventures with local companies to exploit the newly delineated 200 mile zone. Locals have learned a lot about deep sea fishing fleets; one or two big modern trawlers have been built at the Port of Nelson. Research is going into fish farming as well as the development of offshore resources. In the words of the chairman of the Nelson Harbour Board, "Nelson is now the busiest fishing port in New Zealand, both in tonnage and processing facilities." The port has landed the biggest New Zealand wetfish catch for several years. It is also a busy port for foreign fishing vessels. Squid boats and trawlers are frequent visitors, and Japanese, Russian, Korean, Taiwanese crew are a familiar sight around the waterfront and in the city.

Nelson itself, adjacent to Cook Strait fishing grounds and with a long history of commercial fishing and boat building, could well become the national centre of the fishing industry as it develops to take full advantage of the 200 mile limit. Fishery research vessels make Nelson their home, and the Nelson Polytechnic provides courses for fishermen.

Fish farming is being developed. Locals have been granted licences to "farm" shallow inlets in the Sounds and Golden Bay. The green-lipped mussel, unique to New Zealand, is highly praised overseas, and is winning favour in New Zealand. The market has steadied after an initial flourish, but continues to be another active export industry, with processing at Nelson, Havelock, and Motueka.

The Nelson economy has a diversity which has often insulated the province from the worst ups and downs in New Zealand's trade. New Zealand is one of the world's great food larders, and Nelson is well poised to benefit from the likely horticulture boom of the 1980s. The bonus of rapidly expanding forest and fish exports would seem to guarantee continued economic stability, the hallmark of these Cook Strait lowlands ever since the first uncertain years of European settlement.

PART II

Townscapes and Transport Links

There is no metropolis in the north of the South Island. Even the zone from the Glen to Richmond through Nelson city, much the most urbanised area, has a settlement pattern pleasantly broken by hills, or green farm and orchard belts. The north–south drift of the ranges defines areas of settlement quite abruptly, creating a strong sense of community in most districts, as well as the disadvantages of a scattered population pattern and at times strong parochial rivalries. Townships by and large still primarily serve surrounding farmlands—though some now also have a holiday role and one or two are forestry settlements. An unusually nice balance between urban and rural life prevails—one of the region's attractions. Settlements with a wilderness backdrop, either on or never far from the sea, and fringed by farmlands are very appealing places to live.

Nelson city

Nelson city and its immediate environs epitomise the way the region achieves a balance between its "civilised" and "primaeval" aspects. The bush-clad "Doubles" and the barren Dun Mountain rise to over 1,100 m at the city's back door; Nelson Haven and Tahuna Beach lie at its front door. It is no distance at all from the city to a first-class beach, a mountain walk, a river valley pool with a grassy picnicking space; an estuary or a bay.

The most common approach to Nelson is from the north, from which direction the city looks impressive by night and day. Across the expanse of Nelson Haven's tidal flats, the city centre buildings are "on stage" in an amphitheatre of hills. The Maitai River curls through the "stage" to meet the Haven in the south-west corner. A prominent knoll in the centre has become, as Bishop Selwyn forecast in 1842, the "acropolis" for Nelson's cathedral. In clear weather the view extends south across the Waimea Inlet to the Moutere hills, and west across the bay to the lofty Tasman Mountains. The site of Nelson has been much admired since Captain Moore

proposed it as the New Zealand Company's second colony in December 1841. In the words of colonist William Curling Young, who arrived the following January: "At night it is so pretty and pavilion like, and the view from our hill so surpassingly beautiful that we are the envy of all . . . I never dreamed of the beauties of this place. The view of the mountains across the bay is as Italian as possible."

Today Nelson almost does justice to its site. It is an unbustling and uncluttered city with an air of integrity. Surrounding hills and green belts fortunately provide natural boundaries for the town between Atawhai and Tahunanui. The sprawl does not start until Stoke is reached, and then extends only fitfully to Richmond and out onto the Waimea Plains. In many ways Nelson is uncharacteristic of the smaller New Zealand cities, and is as distinct from Blenheim, its Marlborough rival "over the hill", as chalk from cheese. It was bestowed city status well before its due (in terms of population) when in 1858 Queen Victoria elevated the town to a bishop's see. The city's present population is approximately 34,000, and including Richmond it makes up an urban area of about 44,000.

The city has from the beginning possessed two focal points: first, the cathedral and the retail and commercial area, laid out in rectangular pattern with the major street names all associated with Lord Nelson's ships and battles; second, a kilometre or so away around the Haven and under the Port Hills, Nelson's port, nowadays making use of extensive reclaimed land, with street names taken from harbour board, pilot and shipping personalities.

Park gardens, wide streets, hectares of tomato glasshouses right on the edge of the commercial area, and the riverside all combine to create a feeling of spaciousness in the city centre. Foresight on the part of the city fathers some years ago provided two large central carpark squares behind either side of Trafalgar Street. The middle section of Trafalgar Street may soon be turned into a mall to further encourage pleasant pedestrian shopping.

Church Hill was topped by a church from 1843–58, and since then by a cathedral. Built of Takaka marble, the present cathedral has a medieval aspect in both its basic style, and its prominence in the middle of the city. Its modest size and simple elegance suit the city of which it is still visually the focal point. The church steps, presented by Nelson's wealthy benefactor Thomas Cawthron, and modelled on the Spanish steps of Rome, are a graceful link from Trafalgar Street to the cathedral. The grassy slopes facing the sun, and the shady places under long established trees of the cathedral grounds, are favoured by city shoppers and workers as a lunch spot or a place to rest.

One of the surveyors engaged in marking out lines for roads and urban sections for the new township in January 1842 noted the opportunity presented by "the pretty eminences and gently rising slopes for the display of architectural taste". City residences—both the dignified, well-kept old houses still much in evidence and many well-designed recent homes—do contribute much toward the fulfilment of Surveyor Stephens's initial expectation for the site. The sensitivity of many Nelsonians to the style they feel their city possesses was exposed with the recent construction of two uncharacteristically large buildings. Both the Rutherford Hotel near the cathedral in Nile Street, built in the early seventies, and a replacement Chief Post Office completed at the bottom end of Trafalgar Street in 1983, are monolithic structures of eight to nine floors. Protests were made about the dominating height of the new buildings especially the post office, which actually infringed the city council's own height restrictions. City traditionalists must hope that their stylish cathedral, though in some ways now overshadowed, will remain the centre of attention in spite of the rather gross competition provided by a palace of commercial tourism on the one hand, and a temple to bureaucracy on the other.

South of the city

The southern outlet via Haven Road and Wakefield Quay makes a fine marine drive. Tucked along the hillsides are old seaside homes, mostly kept in good condition; the nineteenth century wharves, still in use outside the reclamation, are attractive and a neat chain fence (another Cawthron bequest) runs along the sea ramparts. Above, on the crest of the Port Hills, is Nelson's residential dress circle. These homes have a complete panorama of Tasman Bay and they look down on a foreground of Fifeshire Rock, Haulashore Island, and the Haven's natural breakwater of the boulder bank, on which the now disused lighthouse, second oldest in New Zealand, stands starkly. The view

Haven Road about 1905 (Nelson Provincial Museum, Jones collection.)

is dramatic at any time—in clear blue weather the mountains from Mount Owen to Separation Point stand out over a sparkling bay; in a storm the northerly swell crashes the surf against the breakwater and Tahunanui Beach. Sometimes the most beautiful view of all is when the waters of the bay are brushed in shades of grey with breeze stilled under a leaden sky, so restful to the eye. Most houses are above the rumble of the big trucks along the port road. There is always lively movement of boats, small and large, through the Haven entrance, and the end of the day, when the sun dips behind the Tasman Mountains, often sees a breath-taking sunset.

The industrial zone makes use of flat land south of Tahunanui Beach, around the airport, and in the suburb of Stoke. Construction firms, light electrical supplies, car assembly plant, fruit juice processing, stone and clay supplies, light engineering and freezing works are all well established. At first manufacturing industries were restricted to those not handicapped by transport costs, but now a number of smaller specialist industries, with their eyes on the export market, are moving in.

The alternative route south out of the city passes over the semirural Bishopdale rise, into the Stoke shopping centre, and then quickly out to orchards and farm paddocks again. Stoke-on-Trent gave its name to Nelson's Stoke, just as Richmond-on-Thames was the inspiration for the borough of Richmond, about 12 km south of Nelson city. In Richmond, even in Stoke, horse and rider may be seen exercising on a main street—but it is in Richmond, host to the annual Agricultural and Pastoral Show in November, where town and country really meet. Though becoming mainly a pleasant dormitory town for Nelson, Richmond has its own light industrial zone by the southern outlet, with fertiliser works and timber chip mill nearby. The borough ranks high as an educational centre—the educational complex in Salisbury Road includes Waimea College, the largest secondary school in the province, three other schools, and a kindergarten. Teachers make up a significant part of Richmond's population. Attractive residential areas on the sunny upper slopes, and its urban-rural character, attract retired people. Richmond (present population around 7,000) has been the fastest growing borough in the South Island for a generation, and it is still expanding rapidly. Richmond's shopping centre and large, active mall provide a healthy rivalry to the retail sector of Nelson city, especially for shoppers from the agriculturally rich Waimea Plains.

Other settlements of the Waimea Plains are Brightwater and further out Wakefield, the latter 29 km from Nelson. Though these are still largely rural servicing centres, Nelsonians do commute to both. Brightwater has a dairy factory, and a quarry stone firm. It is also the birthplace of Ernest Rutherford, father of nuclear physics, who received his secondary education at Nelson College and while at Cambridge University was the first to split the atom. Brightwater may well become internationally famous if the powers that be ever get round to devising a fitting memorial to him. At present Rutherford's old home site is almost bare. Historic Wakefield, a larger township than Brightwater, has forestry links through its proximity to Golden Downs.

From Wakefield, State Highway 6 soon reaches the summit of Spooners Range, from where an excellent view north of the Waimea Plains and Nelson is obtained. The southern view shows how the gentle ridges of the Moutere hills (of which Spooners is one) have been used for exotic forestry development. Most of the forest in view is radiata, but larch and other species line the road down from Spooners. The variety of planting, mainly for amenity purposes, is particularly attractive in the roadside development leading to the next summit, Hope Saddle, from which the road drops to the Lake Rotoiti junction at Kawatiri.

There are two other alternative routes to Lake Rotoiti—one starts from a junction just before the Hope Saddle, and passes through Kikiwa; the other leaves the highway back before Spooners at Belgrove, and is the most direct route. This latter passes through Golden Downs, the second largest plantation forest in New Zealand. Near Rotoiti the Tophouse route to Blenheim can be taken, or the lake passed to rejoin the main highway at Kawatiri. From that point Highway 6 truly enters the green world of beech forests and winds its way along dramatic river sweeps of the Buller amidst earthquake-rent mountain sides. At Murchison (140 km from Nelson) is a basin formed by the meeting of several tributaries of the Buller—the Mangles, Matakitaki, Matiri, and Maruia—each with a history of gold rushes, but now mainly fishing and scenic waters, especially in the mountain

reaches. Murchison township is the centre of a dairying and mixed farming district.

The highway then hugs the upper Buller gorges to Inangahua Junction, the road to Christchurch having diverged shortly after Murchison to follow up the Maruia Valley. From Inangahua Junction two routes to the West Coast—via Reefton or via Westport— lead out of the Nelson region.

The great beech forests of the lower hills and terraces of the Buller, Maruia, and Reefton districts are relevant to Nelson, however. Chip mills, as well as the proposed large-scale pulp mill, may depend partly on the milling of large stands of native beech there. The ethics and economics of this are hotly debated. In the meantime Murchison and Reefton are peaceful communities resting on past laurels of gold, coal, and timber, though the tranquillity cannot always be taken for granted as severe earthquake shocks in 1929 and 1968 made clear.

West to Motueka and Golden Bay

Two roads cut across the Moutere hills to Motueka, less than an hour's run from Nelson either way. The most direct is the coastal. Once past the Waimea Plains, Mapua is soon reached by turning back from the main road a kilometre or so to the Mapua Inlet. Established as a fruit outlet, the port is now hardly used, though the township grows as residential sections on the coast become more and more attractive. A large agricultural chemicals factory provides employment in the township, as does the Mapua Leisure Park though in a smaller way. Ruby Bay, a few kilometres further on, consists almost entirely of coastal residences. Above the Ruby Bay bluff is Tasman, the heart of apple country, where most substantial buildings are of the packhouse variety. The road then slips past the lovely inlet between Kina and Mariri to reach Motueka.

The inland route leaves the junction of Appleby to ascend the Moutere hills to Upper Moutere, a village forever framed by the German influence of the 1840s, with a Lutheran Church, oasthouses and vineyards to prove it. The main road then rambles over the crests and vales of the Mouteres until it reaches the Motueka valley at Lower Moutere, a small outlier of Motueka.

Minor roads diverge to the right to link with the coastal highway, and to the left again to ramble over the ridges leading to placenames, but hardly townships, such as Neudorf, Dovedale, and Ngatimoti. There are few more lovely drives than along the by-roads of the Moutere hills. In parts the ridges are still rough with gorse and second growth and derelict houses are reminders of earlier defeat by the

Moutere gravels. More commonly today the undulating ridges present a harmonious picture of rolling pastures, poplar- or willow-lined stream beds, or stands of exotic pine forest. Always there is a different view round the corner—maybe a small school or tiny church on the rise, a vineyard lying to the sun, an old timber mill, a hop oasthouse or tobacco drying shed. Any farmhouse built on the crest of a Moutere ridge gets the full, magnificent panorama: backdrop to the east, south and west is always high mountains, and northwards the ridges roll gently down to the coast and bay.

Motueka, 50 km from Nelson by the coastal route, is the third-largest town in the province, with a population of about 4,500. Its shopping centre is largely built on Maori reserve. Two other interesting features of its early settlement were the large number of retired English army and navy officers among its colonists, and the legacy from the early survey of an extraordinarily long main street. (It shares this characteristic with Richmond, its rival on the other side of the Mouteres, where the long main street on paper actually continues up the rather steep Richmond Hill, and is still fenced accordingly!)

Perhaps Motueka's chief claim to fame is that two of New Zealand's recent prime ministers, Keith Holyoake and Bill Rowling, came from well-known local families. It is a very prosperous little town servicing an extremely fertile agricultural district. The area produces much of New Zealand's hops and tobacco, but many local farmers are diversifying rapidly into other crops such as kiwifruit, boysenberries, feijoas, rock melons, and garlic. Motueka contains an Apple and Pear Board coolstore, freeze-dried factory for processing locally grown vegetables, and two tobacco warehouses. Port Motueka has died for coastal traffic, but its small boat fishing fleet keeps the important local employer Talleys Fisheries in wet fish and scallops for processing. The town is a busy bus and truck stopover on the way to Golden Bay. More sheltered and milder than average, the climate has encouraged retirement housing, strongly evident from Port Motueka around the coast to Riwaka. In summer the shopping centre gets a boost when holidaymakers from various pleasant spots around the district, most notably Kaiteriteri, come to town. At the same time Motueka's population is almost doubled by the seasonal influx of workers as the orchard fruit, tobacco, hops, and market vegetables all come in. The whole character of the town is altered. As Motueka's publicity booklet puts it: "Farmers and bohemians mingle happily, and often overlap at harvest time. Everybody turns to and picks, and 3,000 workers, mainly students, pour into the area, many wearing beards and beads, strolling tanned and tight-bellied through the streets by day and livening the night spots in the evening."

By following up the Motueka valley, travellers can join State Highway 6 again at Kohatu. The

A Motueka Valley farm c. 1887 (Nelson Provincial Museum, Tyree collection.)

route passes through Tapawera, centre for the farming and small berryfruit basin lying where the valley broadens under the bulk of the Mount Arthur Range. Tapawera is now headquarters of the Golden Downs Forest.

Just before the big hill climb to Golden Bay roads go off the main highway to Kaiteriteri (13 km from Motueka) and Sandy Bay, one route going to the right around the coast, and the other across a ridge direct to Sandy Bay. A little further on the left is a road to the source of the Riwaka River.

Between Motueka and these three junctions is Riwaka township. Its economy also based on the rich silts of the lower Motueka valley, Riwaka is a traditional centre of hop and tobacco farming, with a DSIR research station specialising in hop and tobacco problems but also extending into alternative crop research. Early settlers felt the Riwaka Valley was the most beautiful in the colony, and it is still a lovely valley from its strange source where cold clear water rushes directly out of a cave at the base of the Takaka hill to its nicely decadent old port. There are several bush reserves along the valley, and excellent fly fishing and picnicking spots.

Golden Bay is reached over the biggest of all main road hauls in the province. In fact the Takaka hill road is one of the highest through-roads in New Zealand, reaching a summit of 791 metres after nearly 20 km of uphill travel. As the road levels off to a plateau, Ngarua Caves, 20 km from Motueka, are reached. These are Nelson's Waitomo, open to the public and well worth a visit. Superb views of the Tasman Bay lowlands are gained after this point. The road over the summit plateau passes through weirdly beautiful fluted marble "headstones" which poke out of the grassy fields in profusion.

The steep western wall of the "marble mountain" is descended by long zigzags to the valley floor at Upper Takaka. Here is the junction of the Cobb Dam road, a winding 16 km to the high reservoir lake.

Golden Bay valleys collect more rain than Nelson, and their heavier soils have been made into first class dairying and fat lamb country. The road down the valley is rewardingly peaceful after the grandeur of the big hill. Takaka, 57 km from Motueka, is definitely a "one long main street" town. It is surrounded by a very rugged hinterland, balanced by beautiful, gentle beaches to east and west of the township, and has a population of about 1,000. The co-operative dairy factory recently incorporated its neighbour at Collingwood as part of an extensive modernisation programme. It now very efficiently produces mainly butter and casein, but the market is also being tested for other

promising milk by-products. Its bulk milk tankers have become a feature of Golden Bay roads. A few kilometres around the coast to the east is Golden Bay's other major industry, the cement works at Tarakohe. The limestone and marl formations underlying the Takaka marbles produce about 20 percent of New Zealand's cement requirements. From the artificial harbour, considerably improved in 1982, the company's ships *Ligar Bay* and *Golden Bay* distribute the cement in bulk to packing plants in Wellington, Wanganui, New Plymouth, Raglan, and Nelson.

Half an hour's drive westward along the coast is Collingwood, once with all the fascination of a gold town and port, now of interest mainly for those to whom intriguing dead ends are a magnet. The four-wheel drive safari onto Farewell Spit, the long gravel road to the West Coast beaches via Westhaven Inlet, and the road inland to the start of the Heaphy track, all commence from Collingwood. It is, of course, also an excellent holidaying district, offering beaches, camping, tramping and alluvial prospecting around New Zealand's first goldfield.

Golden Bay is a haven for a mixed and lively community of locals, retired outsiders, co-operative or commune groups, and innovative producers of new crops. Persimmons and

Water race for gold recovery on the Aorere field, Collingwood c.1900 (Nelson Provincial Museum, Tyree collection.)

avocado, loquat and feijoa, walnuts and almonds, salmon and mussel farming are all being tried. The versatile if small population fiercely respect the Bay and its life-styles, and are very much of two minds about the advantages of a road link to Karamea which would put them on the main tourist circuit.

East to Picton

To get east the road has you go north. The first link with Picton followed directly east, over the Maungatapu Saddle at the head of the Maitai. The present highway takes off in different directions like a yoyo attempting to find more reasonable gradients between Nelson and Marlborough. As the crow flies the distance from Nelson to Picton is about 60 km; by main highway this stretches out to 138 km. At Hira a side road goes first to Cable Bay (landing place for the first trans-Tasman telegraphic cable) then Delaware Bay (with its interesting Maori history and its association of Huria Matenga's rescue of sailors shipwrecked in the *Delaware*). Once across the Whangamoas another road turns off to Kokorua and the Whangamoa estuary. These are both interesting short trips, but neither Delaware Bay nor Whangamoa has public road access to the beach.

The Whangamoa Saddle, quite a long haul, is followed by the lower Rai Saddle, where long established slopes of exotic forest (some now being logged) are passed through to reach Rai township (49 km from Nelson), centre of a dairy farming community and junction for the French Pass road. Soon reached is the delightful Pelorus Bridge camping ground, set in mixed native forest where the old Maungatapu trail rejoins the main highway. Just a step further on comes Canvastown—apart from hotel, store and school, merely a ghost town of the Wakamarina gold rush days.

Finally the highway, which until now has skirted the Sounds country without a glimpse of a waterway, meets the southern arm of Pelorus Sound before Havelock.

Wakamarina gold fever gave birth to this township 76 km from Nelson, but its harbour is too shallow for a large port, and today it contents itself with servicing the holiday fishing fleet and other requirements of Pelorus Sound as far round as French Pass and D'Urville Island. Tony Nolan in his *Gold Trails of Nelson/Marlborough* credits Havelock (population about 300) with "an air of tranquil maturity". This description does justice to the many old buildings on the hillslope, the nineteenth century façades along the main highway, and to Havelock's peaceful old wharf.

By now the traveller is well into Marlborough, for Nelson shares the Sounds with its neighbouring province. However, a description of routes in and out would not be complete with a mention of Picton, so often the gateway to the Nelson Province. From Havelock there are two ways of reaching Picton—one is to follow the main highway south through the Kaituna gap to the Wairau, bypass Blenheim direct to Spring Creek, and turn back north through another gap to Picton. The alternative is a much shorter, more scenic, but winding road which takes about the same travelling time. From Havelock the road crosses Cullen Point into the Linkwater Valley, then follows the bays of Grove Arm and Queen Charlotte Sound to Picton. Beautifully set off by bushed hills at the head of Queen Charlotte, Picton (population about 3,500) is the South Island terminal of the interisland road and rail ferry, and a town traditionally geared to travel and holiday industry.

Transportation

Roads have meant more to Nelson than most parts of the country. The South Island trunk railway system never made it to Nelson. Given the topography of the province not a wide choice of alternative land routes existed. Once coastal shipping became insignificant, the few major land routes became lifelines, and good road services the indispensable prerequisite to growth. Nelson has been fortunate that the latter have more than measured up. Perhaps the size of the challenge creates the quality of the response.

For the first decades of settlement the sea was the obvious highway. During the gold rush period of the 1860s and 70s, dray roads were slowly extended by pick and shovel work, and public transport in the form of bullock wagons and coaches began to rattle or squelch along the routes. Land links for the first century posed all sorts of difficulties to engineers and politicians. The road south especially has offered great engineering problems and twice in this century— in 1929 and 1968—the middle section through the Buller gorge has had to be almost completely reconstructed after earthquake upheavals.

Nelson's railway history started with a brief burst of glory when the Dun Mountain railway, albeit horsedrawn, carried passenger traffic from port to city on the first leg of its haul up the

The port to city tram outside the Ship (Tasman) Hotel c.1895. (Nelson Provincial Museum, Tyree collection.)

Dun Mountain in 1861. This gives Nelson claim to have constructed the first railway in the country. When the national railway building boom inspired by Julius Vogel commenced in the 1870s, it was not a question of whether to join the railway system, but of which way to go—over the hills to Wairau, thence to Picton and Christchurch; or through the Buller gorge to the West Coast gold and coal districts.

After much survey and debate the latter route was chosen. Nelson's railway dream progressed in fits and starts. The first section to Foxhill, about 30 km south of Nelson, was completed in 1876. By 1912 the line had reached Glenhope, about 90 km south—and there it stuck for nearly half a century, with another 90 km to be completed before a link could be made at Inangahua Junction. To the sorrow of most Nelsonians and against loud public protest, the rails were dug up in 1956. Nelson's railway history ended indeed as a tale of sound and fury, signifying nothing.

This seemed a disaster at the time—but lack of railway progress had spurred one of New Zealand's most remarkable land transport sagas.

During the 1870s—against all the odds that long distances, dangerous rivers and one of the most difficult of all routes in a country of impossible topography could throw at them— two Newman brothers, Tom and Harry, tried to establish a coachline into the Buller gorge. By dint of the quality of drivers, coaches, horses and service, a coachline became established. The Newmans cut their cartage teeth with timber and supplies to the upper Buller goldfields, but were soon carrying passengers and "Her Majesty's Mail". In 1879 the brothers won the contract for a fortnightly passenger and mail service from Foxhill (terminus of the new railway) to Hampden (Murchison).

This was a big step forward in the success of a road passenger company which for generations now has carried Nelson travellers—at first in four-horse-and-coach style, when in sunny weather passengers could take a spell walking to enjoy the pleasures of the birds and the bush in the Buller gorge; next in early motor vehicle days, installed in a quality Cadillac; then came sturdy Leyland buses, and finally the comfortable sleek 45-seat Mercedes and Volvo aluminium tourers of recent years.

Newmans Cobb & Co coach on the summit of Hope Saddle c.1893 (Nelson Provincial Museum, Tyree collection.)

Today Newmans coaches run daily services from Nelson to Christchurch (both Lewis Pass inland route and Kaikoura coastal route); link the Picton ferry to Christchurch; link Nelson with the West Coast via Westport to Greymouth; and run a daily service over the hill to Takaka. They also provide a fast service for light freight. While the company retains its reputation for friendliness "Newmans" has become a by-word for quality and efficiency. The special care and attention to vehicles and drivers that has been associated with Newmans since the first "coach and two" trip in 1879 is still a feature of company policy.

Newmans extended their bus service into the North Island between the wars, and since World War 2 have entered the national coach and motor caravan and holiday business where they are now the market leaders. The Newmans coach fleet exceeds 150 vehicles. With characteristic initiative, the company has built up contacts and offices overseas, for example in Japan and Australia. However, Newmans remains an institution inextricably woven into the past and present land links in the top half of the South Island, where its name has the stuff of legend about it.

In 1973 Newmans became merely one part of a very big (by New Zealand standards) transport combine. Private heavy road transport developed early in the Nelson Province, and by 1938 twelve firms of "truckies" saw the merits of combining— the result was Transport (Nelson) Ltd. The Government's "notional railway" subsidy rate, established after the railway was closed, and the rapid upgrading of highways, helped the new company into the era of the "big rigs". The combine prospered under local leadership, soon becoming the biggest trucking firm in New Zealand.

Through the 1970s the firm built up a network of interests throughout the province by incorporating Newmans, Lime & Marble (a firm involved in mineral exploration and agricultural minerals), Highways Construction and several other truck firms. TNL Group became the parent company of a large number of subsidiaries. The group has developed not only national interests, but made significant overseas earnings. TNL Export Ltd was established to facilitate the export of berryfruit and other horticultural products, and can act on behalf of a wide range of exporters.

TNL's low key but impressively designed building and landscaped grounds (near Nelson Cathedral and Newmans Depot), is headquarters for a group that is still the biggest transport operator in the country, and an enterprise which plays a patently large role in the economy of the province. Recent proposals (not all necessarily proceeded with) have ranged from kiwifruit farming in Karamea, green-lipped mussel export, and Cook Strait hydrofoil services. With its efficiency and resources, TNL is well placed to take another step in the Nelson tradition of road ahead of rail with the recent removal of the 150 km limit on long haulage throughout the country.

Indeed TNL is well situated for any new venture, whether on its own, with another local company such as Baigents (the largest private forestry company in the region), or with New Zealand-wide companies. Total turnover and profit have been consistently high, and efficiency has been recognised by the company's winning several national awards for the presentation of company accounts. With staff numbers approaching 2,000, TNL has become a New Zealand giant, based on Nelson enterprise.

The firm has never lost the common touch or local empathy, however. This is perhaps best illustrated by the fact that when Newmans had their centennial in 1979, it was made into a provincial occasion. The whole proceedings were presided over in characteristic genial fashion by the active septuagenarian Sir Jack Newman, son of founder Tom Newman, and an early chairman of TNL. The occasion was organised with efficiency and style, as befitted the company. Highlight was a grand parade of vehicles of the past, recreating the original journey from Foxhill to Murchison. Two years previously Sir Jack had been knighted for "services to transport, sport and the community" by his Nelson educated and politically blooded compatriot, the new Governor General Sir Keith Holyoake.

The Newman saga and TNL's enterprise have each rated a full-scale book. The Newman story is well told in *High Noon for Coaches* by J Halket Miller and Graham Spencer, and that of TNL by Temple Sutherland in *Nothing to Sell but Service*—both highly readable accounts of the inland roads and the farms, goldfields, and mills they served.

Today there is not a train in sight in the Nelson Province, a circumstance to which TNL—and perhaps Nelson—owe a great deal in that both gained a head start in the era of truck and bus.

Port and airport

Perhaps the best place to observe the scope of TNL operations is on the Port of Nelson reclamation, where much of their heavy fleet is based and where there is a constant rumble of articulated big rigs, chip liners and logging trucks.

The volume of trucking is not the only impressive feature of Nelson's port. Although in contrast to Marlborough's port of Picton it has had no passenger traffic since the Wellington ferry last sailed in 1953, the port is a bustle of shipping activity.

Nelson Haven was adequate for the days when sailing ships slipped through the gap between Fifeshire Rock and Haulashore Island into the shelter of the boulder bank to tie up at the old wharf on Haven Road. The "cut" put through the Haven's remarkable natural breakwater in 1906 saved the port from the effect of shoaling that was occurring at the old entrance, and allowed larger steamers to enter. The cut was widened after World War 2, and by 1951 overseas ships could uplift some of Nelson's exports for the first time. A large reclamation programme then added commercial space and longer wharf berthage. The reclamation is now being extended again in the north side of the Maitai channel, and the recent purchase of a larger tug, the *Huria Matenga*, has allowed for ships of 35,000-plus tons to berth. The present depth of the channel (about seven metres) is likely to be extended to about 10 metres.

Thus an active harbour board has usually been sufficiently flexible and visionary to keep ahead of requirements, and the Port of Nelson is undoubtedly a modern success story. Reclaimed acreage has created space for a wide variety of light industry and service installations; fish processing, shipbuilding, a cement silo, coolstores, oil tanks, chip and log piles, transport yards, and general warehousing, as well as new wharf space for large overseas vessels, a fishing fleet, and a marina for pleasure yachts. Large-scale exports of timber products and fruit are the basis of overseas trade, and Nelson is New Zealand's biggest fishing port. While fish accounted for less than 3 percent (in 1983) of the total tonnage handled, 18 percent of the harbour board's income is from various sources of the fishing industry compared with 26 percent from forest products and 9 percent from the fruit industry. Roll on-roll off service to Australia has recently been provided for. The port has the fastest turn-around in New Zealand and is probably the most mechanised among secondary ports. The bulk loading characteristic of the port is indicated by the statistics for 1983 when Nelson exported 505,000 tonnes—more (by quantity) than any other South Island port, although other ports had considerably higher exports in value.

The narrow "cut"—the only harbour entrance—is a lively sight most days. It is a rare occasion when some type of vessel is not moving through: small yachts or runabouts; tugs or pilot launch; fishing trawlers and research vessels; container, timber and oil carriers; the world's trade and bay's pleasure from the grace of tall

yachts to the squat Japanese squid boats, resembling ancient Roman triremes.

It was easy for Nelsonians to grasp the attractions of flying when mountain ranges or Cook Strait were the obstacles to travel in all directions. Since the loss of the Wellington ferry service in 1953, air services have grown steadily. Another factor was probably the convenient siting of Nelson's airport within the city boundary. This airport is now the fifth busiest in the country for internal flights. As well as Air New Zealand "Friendship" direct flights to Wellington, Christchurch, and Auckland, two companies, Air Albatross and Avcorp, provide competitive services by smaller plane to different North Island centres, as well as Blenheim. A general freight service flies via Blenheim to Wellington, and many of Nelson's perishable products are flown to other parts of New Zealand or overseas.

Nelson, Motueka, and Takaka have their own aero clubs. There are landing strips for light planes in many unlikely places, some for aerial topdressing purposes, some at recreational spots such as Awarua, Lake Rotoiti, and Bainham. Float planes usually use the Sounds as a home base. The two smaller commercial companies, especially Air Albatross with a 16-seater "Metroliner", are likely to tap the tourist market with direct flights from other tourist centres to some of Nelson's recreational areas.

In the past 20 years helicopters have taken a leading role in servicing the province's hard-to-reach spots for deer recovery, forestry and national park supplies, hill country agricultural purposes, and the more publicised search and rescue operations. A Nelson-based firm, Helicopters New Zealand Ltd, ranked as the largest private helicopter firm in the country for many years. Its operations are nationwide, and the company has built up a tremendous pool of experience in the use of helicopters for agricultural and mountaineering purposes, venison recovery, and in recent years for servicing offshore Cook Strait oil exploration rigs. The number of light planes and helicopters available makes a lift into the sky a fairly common work or holiday experience in Nelson.

Transport hardly seems a problem in the 1980s. Upgraded highways, an efficient pattern of trucking and bus passenger traffic, and a flight time to Wellington or Christchurch of less than an hour from Nelson airport are enough to demolish most feelings of isolation. The valley settlement syndrome survives however—kept alive partly by memories of the difficulty of getting in and around in the "good old days".

PART III

Mountains and Marinas

The bane of early settlements—ruggedness of mountain ranges and long coastal headlands—now seems a blessing for Nelson in this age of population pressure. No other New Zealand region can match the impressive total of two national parks, one maritime park, and two major forest parks—all to be reached in a drive of no more than an hour or so from Nelson city. It would be a pity to visit the area and depart without becoming acquainted with at least one of these magnificent natural environments—and these days many overseas visitors do come just to taste outdoor life, Nelson style.

Nelson's extensive mountain lands offer easy access, and the peaks, lakes, rivers, and caving systems are ideal training grounds for mountain activities. In the mountain block east of Nelson, the ridges of the Sounds (which run predominantly north-east to south-west as do all the main ranges) merge into much higher ranges in the Mount Richmond Forest Park. Mount Richmond (1,760 m) and Red Hills (1,790 m) are the highest peaks. This mountain massif terminates abruptly at the southern end in the giant cleft of the Wairau Valley, following the straight edge of the major South Island alpine faultline. A clear demarcation also exists where these mountains meet the eastern edge of the Tasman Bay lowlands.

South of the Wairau Valley and Tophouse, a higher and much younger mountain mass soars to the 2,200-metre-plus summits of the Spenser Mountains. These are in fact the northern terminus of the Southern Alps, sharing their characteristic deep glaciated valleys, shingle screes running into beech forests, alpine summits and winter snows, while benefiting from more reliable weather. From the Spensers eastward, line upon line of bare and dry high country ridges fill the skyline until the Kaikoura Ranges on the east coast block the view.

West of the Buller gorge and Tasman Bay lowlands is the third extensive mountain zone. The granitic tableland of Abel Tasman National Park and the older rocks of north-west Nelson fuse at the head of the Takaka Valley into a single mountain block, its eastern fringe edged with marble from Takaka Saddle to Mount Owen. Westward is a sequence of ridges of striking height conformity, ancient works of infinite geological variety, including some of the oldest rocks in New Zealand. The ridges are split by deeply gorged rivers such as the Mohikinui, Karamea, and Heaphy as they fight their way westward to the ocean.

The major areas of mountain recreation—one in each mountain block—are the Nelson Lakes National Park, the North-West Nelson Forest Park, and the Mount Richmond Forest Park. The Abel Tasman National Park, though better known for its marine attractions, links mountain and sea recreation—very different worlds but matched to perfection in close proximity within New Zealand's smallest national park.

Nelson Lakes National Park

Drive south through Golden Downs State Forest of via Motupiko Valley and in under two hours you reach the Nelson Lakes, where the ranges are alpine, two well organised ski fields (one club and one commercial) operate in winter, and summer holidaymakers can tramp, fish, boat, swim or hunt. The north shore of Lake Rotoiti contains St Arnaud township with the national park headquarters, a store, many holiday cottages, and two camping grounds. The recent formation of a second ski field has encouraged the expansion of tourist facilities there—a motel lodge and restaurant. Rotoiti Lodge, the largest outdoor education centre in the province, stands on a knoll above the township.

Constituted in 1956, the park is based on the attractions of the sister lakes Rotoiti and Rotoroa and the mountainous ranges leading south from them. Geologist/explorer Julius von Haast and lawyer/explorer W L T Travers had much to do with the nomenclature of the area during the 1850s and 1860s. Haast named Mount Franklin after the Arctic explorer, considering it to be the highest peak in these ranges (which it probably is by about a metre). He also named the D'Urville,

Sabine, and Travers rivers; and Mount Robert after his German-born son whom he never saw. Travers gave the general name of Spenser Mountains to the alpine system north of Lewis Pass. Edmund Spenser's long poem, *The Faerie Queene*, inspired many of the names for its peaks and lakes. The St Arnaud Range was named by Travers after a French general of the Crimean War.

Both lakes Rotoiti and Rotoroa lead the eye and the traveller gently into the heart of the park—the high peaks of the Travers, Sabine, and D'Urville valleys. Water taxi services are available to the head of each lake, and the lakes are the usual access to the valley systems. Alternative entries are from Lewis Pass in the south, or from the Wairau–Hanmer hydro road, which can give quick access from the east to some parts of the park. The ranges are snow covered in winter but almost bare in summer, thus there are no glaciers. The valleys generally provide enjoyable, easy walking through well-tracked beech forest and open parkland. Established tracks have good huts, and passes are not too difficult. Well-equipped trampers can carry on south past the delightful Blue Lake and Lake Constance in the West Sabine Valley, and over the Waiau Pass to reach the summit of the Lewis Pass road after a five-to-six day tramp. The peaks are a pleasure to look at, and offer a few challenging climbing routes. The old park handbook, maybe tongue in cheek, categorised the ranges as a "middle-aged mountaineers' mecca". Be that as it may, it is an excellent area for initiating the novice, and on many peaks it is possible to experience a sense of great height without much technical difficulty.

There are invigorating day walks and climbs from the township onto the St Arnaud Range, round Lake Rotoiti, and above the bushline on Mount Robert across the lake. On all walks there is much scope for favourite national park pastimes of botanising, birdwatching, and admiring the views. Mount Robert makes a fine vantage point. Around it pivot the major river systems of Nelson and Marlborough. Looking east through Tophouse Saddle the course of the Wairau River is visible almost as far as Blenheim. North from Mount Robert the Tasman Bay lowlands are laid out at your feet in a dramatic altitude drop caused by the alpine fault, which traverses the base of the mountain. The Motueka River winds across the lowlands finally following their western edge to Tasman Bay. Westward the Buller River escapes from Lake Rotoiti, eventually disappearing into bushed gorges on its way to the West Coast. South, extending to beyond the horizon, are the 2,000-metre-plus ridges of the park, and from their mountain fastness rise not only the Buller and the Wairau, but also the Clarence and the Waiau rivers.

The local ski club has developed its ski field just beyond Mount Robert, in a basin which gives a great variety of skiing. There is as yet no road access, though helicopters are used. The club has a long tradition of active building programmes, planned ski-school weeks, and instruction. Weekend visitors are welcome, and ski gear can be hired. The commercially run Rainbow ski field is located high on the St Arnaud Range, on the opposite side of Lake Rotoiti. This new field with direct road access from the township of less than an hour's drive, has considerably stimulated skiing in the district for it remains open all week.

In summer there is fun to be had with boats of all sorts and sizes on the two lakes and water skiing on Lake Rotoiti. Yachting, a power boat regatta, and a jet boat rally usually take place on Lake Rotoiti in January and February.

Trout fishing is excellent in both lakes, as well as in the Travers, Sabine, and D'Urville, in reality the sources of the Buller, itself a famous fishing river. At the outlet of Lake Rotoroa, a 1920s fishing lodge has recently been restored to provide homely but nevertheless high-class accommodation for New Zealand and overseas fishing enthusiasts. At Lake Rotoroa the climate is milder and the bush more varied. The lake and its Gowan River outlet are immediately at hand for fishing, and several other top fishing rivers within a few kilometres provide all the angling anyone could want. The Nelson Lakes district has the potential to become a world-class trout-fishing centre.

Red deer and chamois are hunted as noxious animals in the bush and tussock basins of the park. Gold is not found within the park, but the Howard, Gowan, and main Buller rivers just outside it contain plenty of prospecting gravels.

Nelson Lakes National Park, including a recent extension towards Lewis Pass, covers 95,505 ha. While smaller than most New Zealand national parks, it possesses very well-balanced mountain resources. Resident rangers are the best source of up-to-date information on this and all the national parks. Information on each park is available from park headquarters, Lands and Survey offices, and city bookshops.

The forest parks

The two forest parks are large areas of reserved land, even by New Zealand standards. North-West Nelson is the largest forest park in the country, and exceeded in area only by Fiordland and Urewera national parks.

Travel the Nelson–Blenheim highway via Havelock and Picton to Blenheim, return via Tophouse and Golden Downs and you have encompassed virtually all 182,000 ha of Mount Richmond Forest Park. The Pelorus Valley dominates the centre of the park, separating the Bryant Range on its west from the higher

Richmond Range. The south-east ridges of this range, truncated by the alpine fault, drop startlingly quickly to the Wairau Valley. Cleared lower ridges around the circumference of the park have been turned from poor grazing land into radiata afforestation, but the heart of the park is native beech forest and, above the bushline, alpine meadowland. More mixed bush prevails in the lower Pelorus Valley, seen at its best in the scenic reserve at Pelorus Bridge. There is an unusual treeless zone along the western mineral belt from Red Hills to Dun Mountain.

The park is easy to get into from either Nelson or Blenheim, and access to many tracks has been speeded in recent years by forestry roads. Good tracks lead into grand tramping, fishing, and shooting country. The most popular trips are from Nelson over the Dun Saddle to Pelorus; from there going upstream to complete a round trip via Totara Saddle; downstream to Pelorus Bridge; or traversing Mount Richmond to exit into the Wairau. The Wakamarina–Wairau route is well used also. Mount Fishtail, Mount Richmond, Mount Patriarch, Red Hills, Ben Nevis, Starveall, and Dun Mountain are all especially fine viewpoints. The Pelorus Valley is a versatile recreational area with swimming, fishing, and canoeing in the river as well as many tramping tracks. It is used extensively for outdoor education, by primary schools (who have a base at Pelorus Bridge), by secondary school tramping parties, and by the Anakiwa Outward Bound school, especially for canoeing. There is only one lake (Lake Chalice), but plenty of bush and valley variety. The Forest Service have devised a number of instructive short walks in Hira Forest near Nelson for the interested short-term visitor to gain views of, and acquaintance with, native bush. The Dun Mountain walkway, making use of the old railway track for about 10 km, fulfils the same role. Many streams in the park repay a little prospecting, especially the Wakamarina where mining claims still abound.

North-West Nelson Forest Park is more remote and covers a vast 376,000 ha of fascinating variety from the wild surf of the western coastline where mountains meet the rolling ocean, to the striking marble ridges of the eastern edge seen from Nelson. Extensive beech forests or tussock tablelands cover the east and north. Subtropical rain forest and nikau palms line the western shoreline, and a wonderfully distinctive alpine scrub and meadowland are displayed above the bushline (where a large number of plants are unique to North-West Nelson). The geology of the park is unbelievably kaleidoscopic. Notable among the baffling variety of rock types (many highly mineralised) are the oldest fossil-bearing rocks in New Zealand. Limestones of the Cobb Valley, dated by the trilobite fossils found in them, are 530 million years old.

Despite this park's complex and rugged topography, gold diggers combed it all last century—as trampers, foresters, fishermen, and mineral companies do now, many however with the aid of a helicopter. Apart from the acclimatisation of trout, deer, and oppossums much of North-West Nelson still has a primaeval feel about it. Access is by no means as direct as many parts of the Nelson/Marlborough back country, and journeys across are more like expeditions. One area is so remote that it has been proposed as a "Wilderness Area" to be retained in its natural, unspoilt state.

The nationally known Heaphy track cuts the north-west corner of the province between Collingwood and Karamea. Hundreds of people each summer complete the 77 km, four-to-five day walk over a track of remarkably even gradient. Since the park was established, the Forest Service have updated the huts and much improved the century-old track. The walk provides a neat trinity of landscape experiences: relatively open beech forest in the climb from the Aorere valley to Perry Saddle hut; red tussock and herbfield over the centre Gouland Downs portion; and lush subtropical rimu, nikau, and rata forest in the lower Heaphy Valley from Lewis Hut to the river mouth and down the final beach walk. Neither end is particularly accessible, but both can be reached by car, taxi, or light plane.

Innumerable trips and climbs are possible in this park. The Wangapeka track makes a satisfying return walk from Karamea for those who have time left after the Heaphy. It consists of a 50 km, three-to-four day trip over rather higher saddles and more difficult terrain than the Heaphy. Routes beyond the easier tracks, which generally follow old gold or stock trails, are often very strenuous. The most familiar peaks to Nelsonians are Mount Owen, the Twins and Mount Arthur, their broad marble summits rising to around 1,800 metres on the western skyline across Tasman Bay.

Fishing is sometimes almost too easy, especially in the earthquake dammed middle reaches—the "bend" area—of the Karamea River, which drains a third of the park. But "too easy" is not a label that could be applied to exploring the cave systems being opened by the spelaeologists in the marble formations of Mount Owen and Mount Arthur. Once again, for those in search of elusive gold there must be few streams without some. North-West Nelson, it must be said, has more than its fair share of bad weather and bleak isolation on the tops, sandflies and floods in the valleys. It is challenging country for any purpose.

Entry to the park is most commonly by the Graham Valley road to Flora Saddle, giving access to the Mount Arthur tableland; or alternatively by the Cobb hydro road into the upper Cobb. Both roads gain almost the first 1,000 metres of height.

Many forest park valleys have become more accessible by dint of the work put into huts and tracks by the New Zealand Forest Service. There are new forestry roads which now make feasible (for fit parties with all-weather clothing) one-day climbs of two outstandingly panoramic peaks. The Graham Valley road to the Flora Saddle carpark gives straightforward track access to Mount Arthur or further on the Twins and a superb view over Tasman Bay, the lowlands, and across the western mountains. Mount Richmond can also be climbed in a day from the Wairau via Top Valley Stream. From its summit an even better panorama is gained, encompassing the Wairau Valley, Kaikouras and Spensers, the Sounds, Tasman Bay lowlands, and the Mount Arthur Range—in other words, most of Nelson/Marlborough.

Forest park rangers are stationed in various parts of the parks but attractive, informative track brochures, or up-to-date information are most easily obtained from the New Zealand Forest Service in Nelson.

Abel Tasman National Park

Take a little over an hour's drive west, then turn north past Motueka and Kaiteriteri to Marahau and you drive no further. From where the granite ridge pushes out towards Separation Point, it is either boating or walking. The coastal walk is easy enough for everyone, from beach to beach of the golden sand for which the park is chiefly famous. By contrast, inland travel can be very difficult. From the tableland summit, rivers cascade 1,000 metres through broken gorges of waterfalls and clinging bush in frightening haste to get to the sea.

It is marvellous coastline for boating, fishing, walking, snorkelling, or just lazing about. The only road into the park is from Takaka to Totaranui. Golden sand is first met at Ligar Bay and Wainui Inlet. Then a narrow road winds throught a remnant of virgin rain forest over the big hill to Totaranui. Here, within the national park, is a superb camping ground, large and informal enough for those who don't need too many facilities to enjoy the safe swimming, fishing, tramping, boating, and beach life. At Totaranui are resident park rangers and the visitor centre. (The park headquarters is actually at Takaka.) The first stretch of coastal walk takes you to the Awaroa estuary and beach; then come Tonga, Bark Bay, Torrent Bay, the little beaches on Astrolabe Roadstead and Coquille Bay—it is impossible to say which would take the prize. Finely sculptured granite headlands, each with a tide-washed reef perfect for rock pools, fishing, and snorkelling, separate the beaches which are like the gems in some dazzling necklace of jewels draped around the central headland of the park.

The road end is met again at Marahau, where there is also a camping ground outside the park and a resident ranger. The coastal walk usually takes two to three days and roomy national park huts are sited at Awaroa, Bark Bay, and the Anchorage at Torrent Bay. A regular launch service from Kaiteriteri to Torrent Bay and Totaranui is the ideal way to solve the return transport problem. Kaiteriteri, only a few kilometres from Motueka and possessing an excellent anchorage, is the easiest access point and supply centre for boats which ply the park coastline.

Abel Tasman has been fairly described as a family park because of its wide range of easily accessible attractions, all within a small compass. It is special in other ways too. It is unique in the national park system in that the primary focus of the park is maritime; there is nothing like its coastal walk in any other national park. It is quite possible to spend most of a holiday absorbed in the conchology, ornithology, and seashore life along the coastal beaches, and admiring how the islands just offshore— Fishermans, Adele, Tonga and the Tatas, bird sanctuaries all—adorn the seascapes. The park is also rich is historical associations; as a witness the Abel Tasman memorial stands just outside its western boundary, at Ligar Bay.

Inland, botany has great variety, being a blending of North and South Island species. All five species of beech tree are distributed in the park, and the whau, or native cork tree, reaches its southern limit there. Park vegetation changes upward from coastal bush species to alpine moorland, and west to east from rain forest to a belt of poor soil manuka scrubland. Forest cover in the headwaters of the Falls and Awaroa rivers remains unmodified by human, deer, goat or oppossum. All rivers other than the Wainui still have only indigenous fish in them.

On the other hand, the extent to which the coastal land has been modified—by burning, attempts at farming, and introduction of exotics like hakea, gorse, and pines—is very unusual in a national park. Burning and grazing have long ceased, so interesting experiments in regeneration are going on, even making use of gorse to "nurse" native tree species.

Farming, milling, quarrying, and coastal shipping virtually ceased by early this century. Subsequently a few Nelsonians who appreciated the natural beauty and quietude of the coast built baches there, reached by boat from Riwaka or across Tasman Bay. Among them were the Moncrieffs, a determined and energetic English couple. They purchased 194 ha of native bush on Astrolabe Roadstead and in 1937 had this made into a private reserve to ensure its preservation.

Mrs Perrine Moncrieff became an amateur ornithologist of note and it was largely her initiative which led to the preservation of the natural heritage she, her family, and friends had holidayed amidst for many years. Inspiration came also from the historical zeal that arose out of New Zealand's centennial celebrations of 1940, and the tercentenary of Abel Tasman's landfall in 1642. As a result New Zealand's smallest national park (18,200 ha) was proclaimed in 1942. Since then all the recreational uses of the park have been brought to the fore.

Emily Host justly titled her book about the area *The Enchanted Coast.* Visitors from D'Urville onwards have been enchanted by it. Most coves and bays, sheltered from westerly weather and shelving quickly into deep water, make safe anchorages. The growing Nelson keeler and trailer-sailer fleet, as well as yachts from across the Straits, increasingly experience the cruising pleasure found there by D'Urville and his successors. One of the latter wrote in 1841: "This was the only part of New Zealand which came up to my idea of the beautiful and the romantic. I must leave you to imagine, for I cannot adequately describe, the beauty of the little nooks on the coast, every one with its little beach of the most beautiful yellow sand, with an impenetrable mass of evergreen shrubs rising in the background, presenting to the eye every shade of the rainbow."

The bays' coastline, and Marlborough Sounds Maritime Park

Golden Bay and Tasman Bay are justly famous for the variety and extent of their safe beaches. West Coast beaches from Karamea to Cape Farewell are almost unswimmable. The eastern shoreline of Tasman Bay, while not as fierce as the South Island's West Coast, to D'Urville's eye resembled it: "lashed by storms from the west, nothing but steep sides… the swell from the west seems almost permanent and renders navigation just as unpleasant and dangerous here, as it is pleasant and safe on the opposite shore".

But between Nelson Haven and Farewell Spit, a marvellous array of beaches exist, encouraging every water activity except perhaps surfing. First—and one of the finest—is just south of Port Nelson, still well within Nelson city limits at Tahunanui. There the long front beach, safe and swimmable at all tides, meets the back beach beside the Waimea estuary, a walking beach with an air of space and isolation. Together they provide a great asset for the city. The grey sands of Tahunanui continue across the Waimea estuary (quite a distance around by road) in the beach fronting Rabbit Island. Here many

kilometres of sand, sheltered from southerly winds by the island's pine plantations, create a very popular beach for young families. Next come the pebble beaches of Ruby Bay and Kina, where beach settlements prevail, though at Ruby Bay a spacious camping ground is located under the Moutere cliffs. The estuaries of the Motueka and Riwaka rivers then intervene for a few kilometres, after which come the golden granites of Kaiteriteri and the national park.

The splendid curve of Golden Bay provides several long, safe, grey-sand beaches. Pohara, east of Takaka, is sometimes claimed to be the safest beach in the country. Patons Rock, Parapara, and Pakawau are all gently shelving stretches of grey sand, and like Pohara each has a camping ground and motels. Collingwood has an attractive beach frontage, while Onekaka offers a pebble beach that is a delight to the rock-hound. The province really does provide a one-stop beach bonanza, plus high sunshine totals to maximise the benefits.

The Marlborough Sounds, though about equally accessible from Nelson and Blenheim, are very much out on their own. For "going down the Sounds", as Nelsonians say, take the Blenheim highway, and as soon as the Gentle Annie rise is passed, the camel-humpy shapes of the Sounds hills come into view. From various spots along the main highway spindly unsealed roads leave to wind along interminable sharp crests of tentacled ridges, which almost—but never quite—enclose the reaches of these long waterways. There are no settlements worthy of the name within the Sounds, and the road travel is so long and tedious that the usual way to reach resorts and isolated farms is by launch— from Picton for Queen Charlotte Sound, Havelock and Pelorus Sound, and less commonly from Nelson for Croisilles or the D'Urville Island harbours. There is only one better way to go than by water—by floatplane from Picton.

The mail boat and other services make a marine highway of the two Sounds, and the number of fishing and pleasure craft to be seen demonstrate that water is indeed the greatest resource of the Sounds. With almost 1,500 km of coastline, innumerable sheltered coves, and dozens of islands the Marlborough Sounds contain some of the country's best boating waters. The bewildering topography and startling beauty of the drowned valleys that have formed Pelorus and Queen Charlotte Sounds can be fully appreciated only from the air, preferably in early morning light as the sun brings ridges into relief.

For generations, guesthouses have made the Sounds places of peaceful relaxation, far from metropolitan life. There are holiday cottages in most bays, often owned by Wellington or Christchurch people. The climate is mild and sunny. Bush walks abound, some of walkway standard. Others climb onto ridges over 1,000 metres and are quite strenuous. Beaches are usually gravelly, sailing winds fluky; but fishing, motor boating, and scuba diving unequalled. There is no better place to get away from it all.

Large stretches of the Sounds are still farmed with the result that a high percentage of the original mixed beech/podocarp bush cover has disappeared. Exotic forestry and mussel farming are encroaching onto ridges or into bays. The concept of a maritime park arose primarily because of the inevitability of conflict between recreational use and economic development in areas such as this. Selective areas for leisure use or of ecological significance have been reserved over recent years, and at present total 45,500 ha. The maritime park is administered by a park board and the Lands and Survey Department in Blenheim. An excellent map of the park has been published by the department.

Both extremities of the coastline of Golden Bay and Tasman Bay are areas of great ecological interest. The reserves at French Pass, D'Urville Island, and Farewell Spit are worth special mention.

To reach French Pass leave the Blenheim highway at Rai Valley and take a characteristically winding road, which follows the western edge of the Sounds. Sixty kilometres later French Pass is reached—but this drive is worth it. The road descends first to Croisilles Harbour and the holiday/fishing settlement of Okiwi Bay. Just past the settlement is Moncrieff scenic reserve which shows the original podocarp/beech forest at its finest. From Elaine Bay turnoff the views get grander and grander, with a steep drop to Pelorus Sound on the right with its bushcover, inlets and islands, and an equally bird's-eye view of rugged bays and cliffs leading towards French Pass on the left. For a few kilometres past Elaine Bay, the road curls through varied and beautiful bush—mixed beech, rimu, nikau, pungas, and coastal species—as good as any still left in the Sounds. The so-called Beef Barrels soon loom up as the guardian rocks of isolated D'Urville Island—an island which at a distance always has an aura of mystery, like some Shangri-La. Historic French Pass is a shivery sight as the tide swirls through the narrow gap, across which a reef runs three-quarters of the way, leaving about 100 metres of clear passage for the current to move between Cook Strait and Tasman Bay. Boats go through at slack water to avoid the fearsome drop in water level and the whirlpools, created when the tidal current is racing through at up to nine knots. Forever associated with the pass will be D'Urville's successful battle to get the first sailing ship—his corvette *Astrolabe*—through the gap in 1827, and the magical but true tale of the dolphin Pelorus Jack "piloting" the Nelson steamer each time it passed that way for more

than 20 years at the turn of the century.

By arrangement a launch ferry will take the visitor to D'Urville Island where there are good bush walks with tremendous views along the crest of the island, old Maori pa and argillite quarry sites, deeply sheltered harbours, and fishing that always lives up to its reputation. At the northern tip of D'Urville stands Stephens Island and lighthouse, sentinel of Cook Strait. Stephens is one of a few remaining island homes of the New Zealand primaeval remnant, the tuatara lizard, as well the habitat for the Stephens Island native frog. Almost all the islands at the outer reaches of the Sounds, including Stephens, have been made wildlife sanctuaries, to be visited only with prior permission.
French Pass and environs is an area of surpassing biological, geological, and historical interest—but rather difficult to get at.

On the other side of the bays, the north-west tip of the South Island is not as isolated, but Farewell Spit is entirely a wildlife sanctuary to which entry is restricted. From Cook's Cape Farewell, north of Collingwood, a seemingly endless sandspit follows a scimitar curve east, then south a little, reaching out 26 km across Golden Bay. It is still growing inexorably at the rate of about 15 metres a year. At the access point to the spit is the Puponga Farm Park. Though management by the Lands and Survey Department is primarily for production, its aim is also to give the public access to points of scenic, archaeological, and botanical note—and a look at Farewell Spit.

The spit is unobtrusive from this direction however, and to appreciate its landform and birdlife the visitor should join an organised four-wheel drive safari from Collingwood to Farewell lighthouse, timed for the tides. Surfcasting opportunities can be taken on the ocean side, and the birds make an interesting study especially over the immense mudflats uncovered by low tide on the inner curve of the spit. Other than by the safari, a visit to the spit requires special permission, for it is sanctuary for a multitude of birds to feed and roost. Each year in March or April the drama of the godwits is played, as they take off in mass formation and wheel towards Siberia on their migration to the northern summer. Many other significant species make Farewell Spit a home, at least for part of the year—the knot, turnstone, oyster catcher, pied stilt, shag, heron and black swan among them. Recently gannets have begun nesting there. In 1971 the spit was designated a "wetland of international importance" by the International Union for the Conservation of Nature and Natural Resources. It is one of only two such reserves in New Zealand.

Other wetlands of value are the tidal flats, or those that have survived harbour reclamation, close to civilisation on Nelson Haven itself. A natural boulder bank of very unusual, if not unique, formation borders the Haven and its mudflats for 13 km. Farewell Spit is formed by the deposition of sand an ocean current carries most of the way along the West Coast of the South Island, then deposits in the eddies created where the Island is rounded. The boulder bank has also been formed by the action of a strong current, southerly this time, along the western shore of Tasman Bay. While it is simple enough to visualise the transportation of fine grains of sand over a long distance, the bank forming Nelson Haven is of water-rounded granite boulders, some very large indeed, rolled from Mackays Bluff at its northern end and neatly stacked to a uniform width of about 50 m into the giant natural breakwater to which the Port of Nelson owes its existence. A walk along the boulder bank is always full of interest for bird, rock, and driftwood studies; a view of the city from the outside; or just for poking about among the curious flotsam and jetsam the ocean allows to wash onto it.

Several other natural phenomena within the province deserve a mention. The Pupu freshwater springs near Takaka pump the largest volume of any in New Zealand. The Buller gorges, carrying more water than any river system except the Clutha, make a spectacular southward exit from the region through turbulent rapids and earthquake slips. The marble formations at Takaka Hill include Harwood's Hole, at 1,000 m long considered the deepest underground cave network in the southern hemisphere—though the "Nettlebed" system of honeycombed caves in similar formations on Mount Arthur, still being explored, are probably deeper.

Acclimatisation, safaris and walkways

Not all enjoyment of open space has to be independent; nor does it necessarily concern only indigenous fauna. Nineteenth-century European settlers attempted to fill what they considered gaps in our native wild environment, sometimes with disastrous results. Nevertheless many of them got a lot of outdoor satisfaction by catching introduced fish, or hunting pigs, goat, or deer. Recently more and more people are taking advantage of commercial safaris or graded walkways to enjoy the kind of areas into which one hopes roads will never go.

The acclimatisation of introduced animals and fish into Nelson has a long history. Three red deer from an English deer park were successfully liberated in Nelson in 1861. From these two hinds and a stag the South Island red deer herd developed. Nelson became the first province to legalise deer hunting when in 1881 a short

Members of the Bush family pose with their trophies following a successful deer hunt c.1895 (Nelson Provincial Museum, Tyree collection.)

season of a month was allowed. Fallow deer are now also common in a few areas but wild deer, though still hunted for sport or captured live for deer farming, have long been subjected to various types of extermination programmes as "noxious animals". Chamois have reached the Spenser Mountains, where these speedy mountain goats can be hunted along the tops. Wild pigs and goats are also fair game. The Australian oppossum, as a prime bush destroyer, is trapped and poisoned, and its skin sold. Duck shooting is available during the season.

By the 1870s the Nelson Acclimatisation Society (founded in 1863) was actively stocking most rivers and lakes with trout or salmon, which a century later are the source of much sporting pleasure. Angling enthusiasts will maintain there is as good rainbow and brown trout fishing as can be found anywhere in such rivers as the Motueka, Buller, Riwaka, Karamea, and Cobb; in the Nelson lakes; and closer to Nelson in the Rai, Pelorus, Maitai, and Waimea rivers.

Commercial development of the outdoors has developed rapidly in recent years as local safari-type firms provide transport, guides, and facilities for "adventure holidays". Tramps of three to four days into the mountains, rafting whitewater rivers such as the Buller, Pelorus, Clarence, and Wairoa, or fishing the backcountry—all are offered regularly. Four-wheel drive vehicles and helicopters are the favoured transport for some trips. Pony trekking can also be arranged.

The motor launch trip from Kaiteriteri around the Abel Tasman coastline is a long-established service, and the launch owners run organised tramps, making use of their own lodge at Torrent Bay. The Pelorus Sound mail-run launch has an even longer tradition. It is available for fishing or scuba diving charter, and services the Sound most days from Havelock. Chartering a yacht opens up tremendous cruising waters—across Tasman Bay to Kaiteriteri and the safe anchorages of the national park coastline; or "up the line" to Croisilles, Greville Harbour and Port Hardy. Excellent sailing is likely in prevailing westerly winds or northerly sea breezes. Outside the line of D'Urville Island–Separation Point, more testing Cook Strait weather can be met; but once around D'Urville or through French Pass, the expansive sailing waters of Pelorus and Queen Charlotte Sounds open up. The Nelson Public Relations Office is the best source of information about commercial facilities for outdoor recreation available in the region.

Recently "Walkways" have been introduced to the district. These provide well signposted, relatively easy walks through areas of high scenic, botanical, or historic interest. They usually require open access to pastoral land over some sections, and are suitable for inexperienced and family parties, as well as enjoyable for anyone who wants a good day or two out. However, all who undertake them should be well prepared and equipped. Cable Bay and Dun Mountain near Nelson, St James in the Spenser Mountains, and Lyell in the Buller gorge are the local walkways so far.

Environmental action and outdoor education

National and maritime park, forest park, state native forest, and scenic reserves in total occupy approximately 60 percent of the Nelson land district. About 66,000 ha are set aside as scenic reserves (3.4 percent of the total area). Landscape as nature made it is today more highly valued than it was a century ago; the primaeval is more of a solace than an opportunity to locate a saleable commodity. Perhaps Nelsonians recognise this more than most, for quite apart from the remarkable proportion of the province in official reserve land of one kind or another, the region has become a national focus for several voluntary organisations whose sole purpose is to disseminate conservationist and ecological principles.

The Native Forests Action Council (NFAC) originated in Nelson. In the early 1970s the group organised New Zealand's largest petition of 340,000 signatures to preserve the Maruia beech forests of southern Nelson when they were in line to supplement the exotic forest resource for a proposed pulp mill. With very limited funding, the organisation has remained active in arranging publicity, fighting legal battles, and organising petitions.

The Native Forests Action Council and other related conservation organisations such as Friends of the Earth, the Royal New Zealand Forest and Bird Protection Society, and Friends of Nelson Haven and Tasman Bay, in 1977 established the Environment Centre in Alma Lane, Nelson, for the strong ecological movement that has developed in the city. At times, political candidates have come from its able, mainly youthful activists. These people have shown both the organising ability to research and publicise issues, and the interest to explore an

area of concern, whether bush wilderness or tidal flat. Two or three have been elected to the Nelson City Council or the Nelson Catchment Board.

The influence of the ecologists was reflected when recently both the Nelson City Council and the Nelson Bays United Council proclaimed their respective zones of responsibility to be Nuclear Weapon Free. Current environmental issues include the Punakaiki National Park proposal; Forest Service management of the Oparara Valley in North-West Nelson Forest Park; Nelson Haven wetlands; Maitai Valley amenities; and reafforestation in the Marlborough Sounds. Present money-making methods combine effective publicity with the selling of pictorial forest calendars, postcards, "T" shirts, and excellent guidebooks to areas of natural landscape concern such as the Oparara and Paparoas.

Finally in this environmental litany, Nelson was one of the first regions of New Zealand to develop outdoor education programmes at secondary and primary level. Rotoiti Lodge, completed in 1968 as an outdoor centre for most of the Nelson/ Marlborough secondary schools as well as for youth groups, uses the resources of the Nelson Lakes National Park. An impressive, large building, the lodge is a credit to the enthusiastic voluntary work and fundraising involved. Nelson College has built its own outdoor centre at Matakitaki Lodge near Murchison. Nayland College made an old school building on D'Urville Island into a base for outdoor edcuation. Centres for primary schools are established at Marahau and Pelorus Bridge, and Abel Tasman National Park Totaranui Education Centre can be used. Assistance for the thorough-going outdoor education programme now established comes from local tramping, canoe and yacht clubs, and considerable use is made of Forest Service and national park huts. Keen support has come from the Nelson Education Board and controlling college councils. Educational opportunities to experience the back country and the bays, almost unheard of not much more than a decade ago, are now taken for granted by a wide cross-section of pupils.

Such are Nelson's environmental assets. Northern New Zealand has its gulfs, marine fishing and sweeping beaches. The south is famed for its alpine peaks, bush, lakes, fiords, and fast flowing rivers. The particular charm of Nelson, for both resident and visitor in need of recreation, is that it encompasses nearly all scenic attractions—and provides the climate to encourage their full enjoyment. Any visitor wishing to experience the New Zealander's birthright of sun, sea, sand, river, lake and mountain will find that Nelson Province contains more than its fair share of all of them.

PART IV

Trends and Traditions

The sobriquet "sleepy hollow" stuck to Nelson for generations. It implied that communications and commerce—in a word "progress"—had passed the province by. That put-down is now given the lie by a surprisingly cosmopolitan Nelson urban area, and a rapid broadening of educational and cultural institutions. Since the 1960s especially, the Nelson region has gained diversity from new industries, and versatility from those who come to retire, to seek alternative life-styles, or merely for the short-term visitor attractions. As for isolation—Nelsonians can now take it or leave it; it can be virtually eliminated or cultivated, depending on one's needs.

Tourism

The biggest development in the province may yet be the holiday industry. Nelson "mainlanders" are friendly, open to visitors, and can see no better kind of resource development than that of inexhaustible, clean, natural attractions. Most visitors to Nelson are motorised, so both the completion of the Haast Pass highway in 1965 and the provision of a Cook Strait car ferry service gave the Nelson holiday industry the impetus it needed about two decades ago.

The six-week December–January summer holiday period is the peak time for New Zealand visitors. They use caravans and tents in motorcamps, rent private homes in the towns, or take baches at the bays. Most settlements provide a motorcamp, though some are situated in choice but more isolated spots. Many motorcamps are on public land and controlled by local or scenic reserve board. A few are commercially run. Pohara, Tukurua, Motueka, Marahau, Ruby Bay, Murchison, Appleby, and Pelorus Bridge are among the most popular of the older established camps; Kaiteriteri is perhaps the most famous.

Nelson city proffers three motorcamps. The Brook and the Maitai are pleasant, smaller riverside camps set in bush. The third,

Tahunanui, is a very large camp and motel complex sited in the angle formed by a long swimming beach on the city side, and a "back beach" beside the Waimea estuary. Covering about 20 ha, and providing a wide range of facilities itself, the camp can also take advantage of sportsgrounds, a natureland, roller-skating rink, model boating pool, BMX track, and a children's adventure playground between the camp and the beaches. The Nelson Golf Club course is in the same recreational complex. Tahunanui's Christmas capacity is about 5,000 campers—undoubtedly the largest camp of its kind in New Zealand.

Kaiteriteri is one of those motorcamps that families tend to return to for a generation or two—a fact attributable mostly to the beauty of the beach and the area's many other attractions, but also to the full facilities provided and the efficiency of the controlling Recreation Reserve Board. The camp, extending over three hectares, can absorb nearly 2,000 campers, part of the summer holiday influx that turns Kaiteriteri from a settlement of maybe 300 permanent residents into a resort of 6,000 or more.

There is a great variety of camping possibilities. Take Quinney's Bush in the Motupiko Valley (about half way between Nelson and Murchison), for example. It is a totally informal small camping ground by the river, with flying foxes and other simple amusements provided by a friendly farmer who finds this one way of putting Christian values into practice. Mapua Leisure Park, on the other hand, is a large (11 ha) commercial "village", which (while also emphasising informal family involvement) is a "dress optional" camp with a wide range of organised facilities and amusements.

Overseas tourists are more likely to arrive on the luxury coach circuit at any time of the year—but more especially in February and March, which often offer the best summer weather. One of the tourist-class hotels or lodges in Nelson is usually a necessary stop for them. As yet visitors from outside New Zealand do not make up a large percentage of the region's long-term holiday makers, but they are steadily increasing. A recent trend has been the number of young travellers (Canadians, Americans, Germans, Australians and others) who arrive, often by hitch-hiking, to tramp the mountain treks or use Nelson as a starting point for exploring the South Island. For them Youth Hostels in Nelson and Havelock are magnets, as well as the camping grounds and national park huts.

For those travelling in their own vehicles, Nelson city has a high density of motel accommodation, and the rest of the province is also generously provided with motels. Recently specialist tourist lodges in the tradition of the comfortable but out of-the-way Marlborough Sounds guesthouses have opened in places such as Lake Rotoroa and Lake Rotoiti.

Attractions there are aplenty to complement Nelson's environment, climate, and people. Local craftware and history, unusual farm landscapes, and a diverse selection of good eating places already qualify; others are being added. Founders Park, a comprehensive reconstruction of old Nelson buildings, services and industries, commenced in 1983 on a site at the northern entrance to the city. It will soon be a tremendous visitor magnet. The Whakatu Marae will eventually stand next to Founders Park as a focus for Nelson's Maori traditions.

Nelson's public relations people quickly perceived the importance to the visitor industry of attracting conferences. The Trafalgar Centre conference, sport, music, and exhibition stadium, seating about 3,500, was built between the city and the port in the early 1970s. This centre, in combination with the Hotel Rutherford, which also possesses its own conference rooms, gives Nelson a full convention facility. The city annually hosts about 45 major conferences, each bringing a wide range of visitors for a few days.

For 20 years the visitor industry has made itself increasingly felt—one could hardly say adding a life-style to the province, but perhaps improving all life-styles.

A cultural centre

Expanding tourism is one of many factors contributing to another trend of the last two decades—a revival of art and craft. In the early 1960s the work of potters such as Davis, Laird, Smisek and Vine made Nelson into a pottery centre. With his son Paul, Jack Laird still runs a very large commercial enterprise at Waimea Pottery, near Richmond, making domestic stoneware and pots for the New Zealand and overseas market, as well as creating his own more personal ware. Today first-class potters can be found almost anywhere in town or country; and there are several successful semi-amateur pottery collectives. Most sell direct to

the public as well as through galleries and shops. The ready availability of good clays helped growth, and the strong tradition of ceramic craftsmanship has benefited award-winning younger potters such as Royce McGlashen and Peter Gibbs. Pottery has become a spectacular growth craft, almost an industry in the region—one estimate put sales at about $2 million for 1983.

Hand-spinning and weaving are other crafts with strength at a cottage industry level. Both "Foc's' le Weavers" and "7 Weavers" are long-established city groups. Nelson Polytechnic has run a full weaving course for some years. Jewellery is another craft practised; especially fine silverware is made in Nelson by Jens Hansen, Gavin Hitchings, and Ben Vine, and there are several other silver specialists. There are woodturners and batik artists, carvers and leather workers, printers and porcelain painters, dollmakers and door painters. Two national craft and art schools meet each year—one run by the polytechnic in August, the other by the Nelson Provincial Arts Council in January. This council, a very active co-ordinating body, published in 1983 a comprehensive listing of craftspeople and artists throughout the region, the first such booklet made available in New Zealand. Subtitled *Guide to the Arts, Crafts and Cottage Industries of Nelson*, it demonstrates an impressive scope of creative output in the province.

Nelson's Suter Art Gallery, emerging out of the Campbell Sunday Schools under the patronage of Bishop Suter in the 1880s, has given consistent encouragement to local artists and craftspeople, as well as housing a valuable permanent collection. In 1979 community fundraising of a scale comparable to that which produced the Trafalgar Centre a decade earlier so reshaped and revitalised the Suter that it is now a beautiful and functional asset for social occasions in the city, in addition to its role of regularly exhibiting the visual arts. An important part of the Suter's permanent collection consists of nineteeth-century landscapes by John Gully, Nelson College art master of the 1880s. The original of "Cook's Cove" in Queen Charlotte Sound by John Webber, donated by early twentieth-century Nelson politician Dillon Bell, is an outstanding single exhibit, as is the portrait of Julia Matenga by Gottfried Lindauer. Toss Woollaston, a local painter recently knighted for his services to art, is represented there by his portraits and a series of landscapes of the crumpled hills around the Motueka valley and Tasman Bay. There is a host of talented younger painters in the district—Jane Evans is one who has made her mark—who receive plenty of support from the Suter, other art galleries, and the community. A recent Suter exhibition of secondary school art was impressive evidence of the work teenagers are producing in the art departments of the various local colleges.

The School of Music in Nile Street is a healthy institution of venerable ancestry, about to undergo a reconstruction programme of its own. A large staff provides a wide range of music tuition, including orchestral, guitar, and jazz. It was for long the only independent music school in the country, though recently links have been made with Nelson Polytechnic. The School provides regular recitals and concerts featuring local, national, and international artists and there is a wide participation in the community, from young to old, in individual tuition, a local orchestra, choral and jazz groups, chamber music, and musical appreciation sessions. The School has one of the most acoustically perfect small concert chambers in New Zealand. Music is particularly strong in all four of the urban colleges.

The old Theatre Royal in Rutherford Street, used for local repertory, opera and pantomime, has also recently been restored. The Nelson Provincial Museum at Isel Park in Stoke, constructed in 1973 with a Maori wing added in 1983, completes a distinguished bracket of community cultural buildings. It is fortunate to hold the biggest provincial nineteenth-century photographic coverage in New Zealand—just a few from its collection illustrate this book. The museum has also built up a particularly full historical reference library, based on one or two extensive private collections, and the resources of the Nelson Historical Society.

Every two years Nelson city's August festival of the visual and performing arts sparks off lively community involvement, and includes a range of activities for children. Each summer holiday period, the community recreation officer organises a "Larks in Parks" programme with much the same characteristics, but geared more for young people.

One wonders why Nelson has such a strong cultural base for a medium-size New Zealand city. Maybe there was an uncommon weighting of the scales from the start towards culture rather than commerce. One-sixth of the income from the original land allotment sales of the 1840s was set aside as an educational and cultural fund. The Nelson Institute—a novel institution which still exists as a cultural and architectural gadfly in the community—was established for "education, scientific and literary purposes" on board one of the first immigrant ships before the colonists even arrived. Its direct heirs are the Public Library, the Provincial Museum, and the Cawthron collection of scientific relics. A number of Nelson's first colonists were cultured, literary and politically aware gentlemen who leavened an often solid pioneer dough. So an early tradition helps—but climate and life-style attractions must be other magnets for the creative craftsperson and artist,

as well as communities of a size that is not overpowering.

There are notable literary migrants, among whom Maurice Gee stands out—a towering figure in New Zealand literature since the completion of his *Plumb* trilogy over the few short years he has lived in Nelson. Three superb chroniclers and raconteurs of the "back-blocks" add to the Nelson literary landscape: Jim Henderson, born and bred on Takaka Hill, author of *Open Country* anthologies, *Swagger Country,* and *Down from Marble Mountain*, his autobiography published in 1983; Temple Sutherland, a Scottish migrant of half a century ago, wrote of the Buller Valley in depression days and of Nelson transport in books such as *The Golden Bush*, which have become New Zealand classics; and Christine Hunt, born and educated in Nelson, who has sensitively recorded the oral history of Golden Bay old-timers in *Speaking a Silence*. The high standard of editorial, and its team of feature journalists, make the *Nelson Evening Mail* a worthy successor to the *Nelson Examiner* of the 1840s, New Zealand's first independent newspaper and a journal of literary quality.

Nelson has inspired a noteworthy output of written history. Ruth Allen's *Nelson—a history of early settlement*, though stopping short at the 1850s, is one of the most scholarly and rewarding of New Zealand's local histories; Ruth Neale's *Landfall Nelson* and *Pioneer Passengers* (accounts of the early immigrant ships) and J N W Newport's *Footprints I* and *II* (narratives of the Nelson backcountry districts) are all distinguished by their detailed research; Tony Nolan's *Gold Trails of Nelson Marlborough* is succinctly entertaining and well illustrated; both J Halket Miller and Christine Hunt have added convincing, highly personalised accounts of episodes in Nelson's past.

The life-style of urban Nelson does have a rather different balance from that found in comparable New Zealand cities. No other medium-size city has as many craft shops, antique outlets, art galleries, jewellers, or variety in eating places—and (surely some sort of cultural level index) Nelson must have more bookshops for its population than any city in New Zealand, a country supposed to lead the world in its number of book retailers!

Provincial education

The significant trends in the region's education in recent years have been the widening scope of the Nelson Polytechnic Institute and the impact of a community education programme. The status of the polytechnic rose dramatically as it extended its courses and proved sensitive to the community's needs as far afield as Takaka, Murchison, and Blenheim. Original courses were mainly industrial and secretarial. To these were added accounting and management; a three-year full-time nursing course; and a nautical and fisheries programme. The nucleus of a craft school has been established with weaving, pottery, and silverware courses; a variety of other studies have been added, such as horticulture, and the diploma of recreation and sport, as well as evening hobby or examination classes. During 1983 about 240 students took advantage of full-time courses at polytech and no less then 6,400 enrolments were registered in a multitude of part-time courses.

Nelson's Community Education Service (now incorporated into the polytechnic) was one of the first in the country. With skilful use of Nelson's community radio station and other media, it had considerable success during it first few years in breaking down the barriers between formal education and the needs of the adult community. Nelson was one of the pioneers in adult literacy programmes and learning exchanges; communication courses and retirement groups; a committee on small business mangement and a budget advisory services. The community education role was to facilitate these and any other community group needs that came to the surface. The result is that continuing education is now widely accepted throughout the province, and an innovative cultural and educational tradition lives on.

Another provincial institution, though more research than education oriented, deserves inclusion here for the place it holds in Nelson's scientific and cultural development. The Cawthron Institute, renowned since its foundation in 1920 for its contributions to the development of Nelson horticulture, is today an independent and highly qualified research institute specialising in microbe research, industrial and sewage waste, soil and food analysis, and environmental feasibility surveys. It has made its mark as a consultant for private, local body and government organisations, as well as gaining a fine professional reputation over the Pacific zone. The institute will have a special brief as planning on a regional scale develops in Nelson.

Two Nelson colleges (boys and girls) long distinguished in the city are now rivalled by the large co-educational secondary schools of Waimea College at Richmond, Nayland College at Stoke, and Motueka High School. Smaller Form 1-7 schools are found at Reefton and Takaka. An indication of scattered communities is the number of area schools, covering both primary and secondary levels, in rural towns— Rai Valley, Tapawera, Murchison, Collingwood, and Karamea—as well as a high proportion of small one-to-three-teacher primary schools within the Nelson Education Board. Nevertheless primary and secondary education does not suffer from the relatively small number of schools. The quality of the schools and the region's attractions draw and keep staff, and Nelson is possibly the least likely region to experience a teacher shortage.

Contrasting life-styles

Isolated valleys, absence of big cities, extensive wilderness, and the craft tradition all combine to make the province a haven for alternative life-styles. "Back to the land" type communities are tucked away in valleys and bays between Croisilles and Karamea. A new wave of immigrants retreating from overseas industrial worlds has provided some settlers, but most are New Zealanders seeking more relaxed life-styles. The Riverside Community near Lower Moutere, an interesting survival of an age before the counter-culture, was founded on pacifist and religious principles in the 1940s.

Alternative life-styles are significant today— boosting cottage crafts, often a factor in environmental battles, and occasionally a lever in local politics. Alternative communities can contribute a variety of activities and "happenings", usually low key but totally social occasions. The end-of-the-year fair at Fairfield, a fine old house set in a hillside among mature trees near the centre of Nelson, is such a "happening". A condemned derelict house a few years ago but now almost completely restored under the inspiration of a voluntary group, "Friends of Old Fairfield", the old house has become a valuable community facility, and the fair already an event on the entertainment and cultural calendar.

Country craft fairs held during January at Pokororo, Neudorf, Gentle Annie, and Wakefield show a similar spirit, and are now well-established outlets for often isolated amateur craftspeople.

Probably even more pronounced is the impact of a very traditional kind of New Zealand migrant. The attraction of the region for retired people is powerful. Coastal housing development from the Glen (north of Nelson) to Kaiteriteri (north of Motueka) is largely a retirement belt for Nelsonians and outsiders. So are some settlements in the Sounds and in Golden Bay. The extra pressure on housing is one reason why Nelson house prices are consistently at the top of the South Island table. In fact the spending power of retired people is a considerable injection into Nelson's even-paced economy as well as contributing to the rather large number of shops and real estate agents. A glance at a population pyramid for the region will immediately show a comparatively high proportion of older residents.

Recreation

Outdoor sports enthusiasts have always been fortunate in the climate, and indoor sports facilities are improving rapidly with the more general use of college and YMCA gymnasiums, Nelson's Trafalgar Centre and Stoke sports complex. Nelson has its share of sporting achievers—the Dixon brothers, Rod and John, in athletics, and Bevan Congden in cricket are examples. Among traditional New Zealand sports, Nelson has never been a top rugby province (despite being the home of New Zealand's oldest rugby club, and the location of the first rugby match, played at Botanical Reserve in 1870). In cricket, however, the province has held the Hawke Cup, symbol of supremacy among the minor associations, more often than any other district. There is a strong national league soccer side. The climate suits tennis, hockey, netball, outdoor bowls, and golf—beautiful golf courses abound. Basketball, volleyball, badminton, and squash are all played in the main centres. Squash is growing fastest, with new courts at Nelson, Stoke, Richmond, and Motueka—either completed or soon to be.

A strong Nelson swimming association received a great fillip in 1978 with the magnificent Nayland Pool Complex at Stoke—one of the best facilities of its kind in New Zealand. In Nelson and Richmond there are athletics and harrier clubs encouraged by the mana of the Dixons, and competitive cycling. A roller-skating rink gets well used at Tahunanui. Trotting and race meetings are on the calendar occasionally at Richmond Park, and a predominantly rural region supports several pony clubs. The "sport of kings" has a long Nelson tradition. The first race meeting was held at Nelson in 1843, and the Nelson Jockey Club was founded in 1848. The Redwood family of Waimea imported racehorses from the 1850s, Henry Redwood junior eventually gaining the title "Father of the New Zealand Turf".

Nelson's recreational forte, however, is in those activities associated with the great outdoors—lake, sea, wild-water river, mountain and air—which have all blossomed since World War 2. Mountain recreations of tramping, mountaineering, caving, fishing, shooting, and skiing (perhaps four-wheel drive and Moto-X should be included among these); water sports of canoeing, rafting, scuba diving, swimming, water skiing, yachting and—leaping into prominence in the last two or three years—board sailing; air sports of gliding, hang-gliding, and skydiving; there would not be many of these that have not been enthusiastically adopted as Nelson sports.

The Toi Toi Valley tennis club c.1900 (Nelson Provincial Museum, Tyree collection.)

Administration and the future

The Nelson Bays United Council, recently constituted to supervise regional development, incorporates Waimea and Golden Bay counties, along with Nelson city and the Motueka and Richmond boroughs. Under the leadership of present chairman, Rob Maling, Mayor of Richmond, and in conjunction with Nelson City, Motueka, and county administrations, the United Council faces quite different problems from those of the New Zealand Company, the Nelson Provincial Government, or the peppery parochialism of the multiplicity of local bodies of the early twentieth century.

Superb recreational resources, magnificent natural assets, and an economic base of diverse products of land, sea, and industry make up the Nelson Province of today—a great place for family living and holiday recreation. With a rich heritage of nineteenth-century history to stand against consistent recent growth; a balance between urban and rural living; an easy availability of mountain and sea resources; a cultural and craft motif to counterpoint less imaginative New Zealand virtues; and a wide variety of occupations and recreations, the ethos of the region has great attractions for the 1980s. After a century of material progress it is the quality of life that now preoccupies this generation.

Administrative issues in the immediate future will surely have as much to do with maintaining the unsurpassed natural resources of the Nelson Province as with developing new ones. The challenge for long-term planners is to make optimum use of an already well-endowed land. A hundred years ago when English novelist Anthony Trollope visited the province, he related how he became "very much in love with Nelson during the few hours I spent there, but it is not the place I would send a young man to make a fortune".

If Trollope sensed that this was a place more for the enjoyment of life than the coining of wealth, then most of today's residents would say "hear, hear!"—and hope that government, local bodies, citizens, and tourists can keep the province that way.

Council staff at the Trafalgar–Hardy Streets intersection c.1900 (Nelson Provincial Museum, Tyree collection.)

Left, Queen's Gardens.
Mid left, an historic school house.
Mid centre, Nelson College.
Mid right, a charming cottage gallery.
Bottom, Trafalgar Street with the Cathedral.

Above, Croisilles Harbour.
Right, Greville Harbour, D'Urville Island.
Facing page: Looking towards French Pass with D'Urville
Island to the left and Admiralty Bay beyond.

Above, Tennyson Inlet.
Right, a sense of humour at Havelock.
Below, an aerial view of Havelock and Kenepuru Sound.

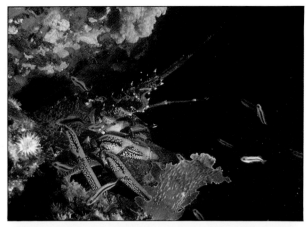

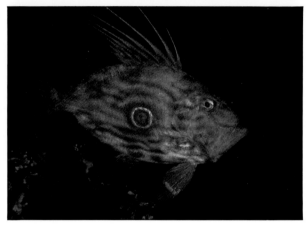

Views of Nelson's prolific underwater life.
(*pictures by D M Boulton*).

Top left, a blue cod.

Left, a jellyfish.

Top right, a crayfish.

Above, a John Dory.

Below, sea eggs.

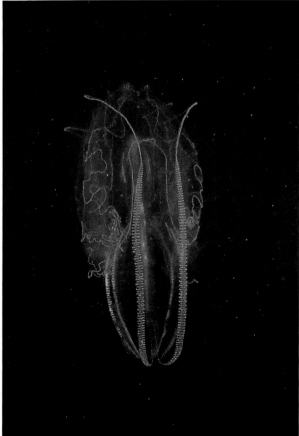

Right, the boulder bank.

Below, a view of Nelson Harbour.

Bottom, a view from the cathedral to the harbour with some of the glasshouses showing in the upper right.

Left, from the Port Hills towards the city centre.
Below, Nelson Haven and the entrance to the harbour.
Bottom, a view of Tahuna Beach.

Two years ago an enterprising young man saw the potential for New Zealand's unique green mussel as a gourmet item for export throughout the world.

John Turner realised that this required the creation of a quality image and an absolute guarantee of the quality of the product. The first was achieved with the registration world-wide of the name KiwiClams and the second objective was achieved with the setting up of a processing facility in Havelock.

His customers in the United States, Japan and Australia can feel absolute confidence that KiwiClams can only come from John Turner. KiwiClams are delivered live from licensed growers to the Havelock plant where they are steamed for three minutes and then opened by hand, graded for size and quality, snap frozen with nitrogen gas and then packed in a protective CO_2 pack to seal in the flavour. John can thus assure his clients that he has control of the KiwiClams from the sea to the supermarket.

He firmly believes that under the KiwiClams concept this unique New Zealand shellfish has an unlimited future and to those who would doubt him he cites the story of the Chinese gooseberry which has gone from an unrecognised horticultural oddity to a $100 million export industry within the space of a few years.

Facing page: KiwiClams country—from the north-east arm
of Croisilles Harbour towards Kenepuru Sound and
beyond.

Top left, Mr KiwiClams: John Turner displays one of his
export packs.

Top right, live KiwiClams on ice at the Havelock Factory
with an export pack displayed amongst them.

Above, KiwiClams being opened by hand.

Above right, the special machine that seals in the flavour.

Some of Nelson's personalities:
Above, Sir Jack and Lady Newman.
Below, Jack Laird.

Facing page: Top, Sir Toss and Lady Woollaston.
Bottom, Sir Toss in his studio.

Facing page: Top, one of Nelson's most popular artists, who also enjoys a national reputation—Jane Evans—at work in her kitchen.

Bottom left, weavers at work at "The 7 Weavers Co-operative".

Bottom right, a display of painted tiles.

Above, John Hadwin outside his studio.

Left, John Hadwin weaving a tapestry.

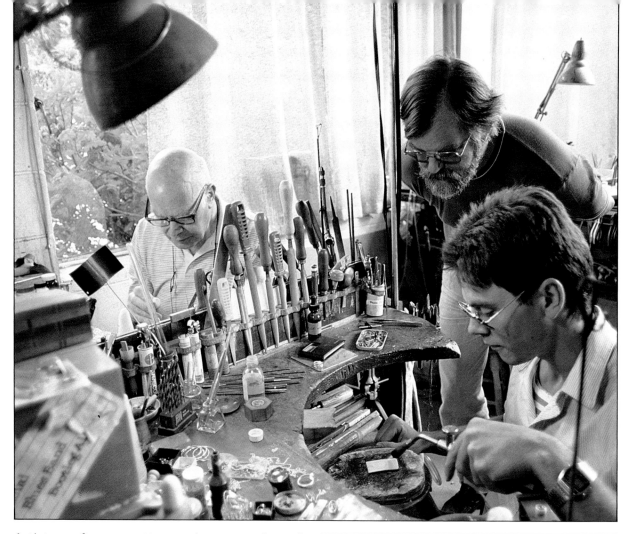

Artists, craftsmen, potters and weavers abound in the Nelson Province and many of them enjoy national status. A good example is the Jens Hansen Silversmith and Goldsmith workshop in Trafalgar Square.

It was founded 15 years ago by Jens Hansen.

Jens began his career as a jeweller 29 years ago. In 1961 he went to Europe for four years and after attending the school of applied art in Copenhagen, worked in various jewellery workshops specialising in individual designs.

He returned to Auckland but in 1969 came to Nelson at the invitation of local backers, including Jack Laird, Douglas Peacock, Graham Kemble-Welch and Heaton Drake.

The new company employed six people but eventually Jens went back to working alone until five years ago when the present co-operative was established.

The members of the group are Jens Hansen, Gavin Hitchings, Ben Vine, Alice Van Halewyn and Tom Harrison.

Top, Jens looks at work being executed by Ben Vine.
Mid right, a display of the finished jewellery
Right, more jewellery.

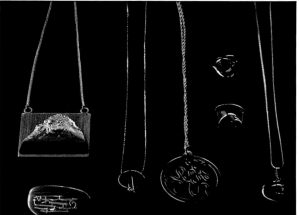

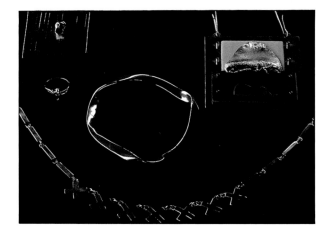

Nelson fairly bursts with potters. At the Public Relations office in the city you can find a list which has some 80 names of potters working full or part-time in the province.

Probably the best known pottery is the Waimea Pottery which was established in 1964 by Jack and Peggy Laird and which continues to flourish under Jack's son Paul, who is the sole producer of Waimea pottery.

During its twenty years of operation the pottery has gone through many stages. During its initial years rising public demand led to increases in staff and then to the establishment of an apprenticeship scheme for potters which has resulted in many potters throughout the country learning how to produce Waimea's distinctive stoneware.

The pottery is situated on the way to Richmond. It has ample parking space and invites visitors to its showroom which features Paul's work as well as the work of other visiting potters who are welcome to use the workshop space and whose pieces give the pottery an international flavour.

Paul works with his wife Colleen and his brother Nick in a separate enterprise which produces decorated tiles. These are designed by Nick and handpainted by Colleen. They are called krocatiles.

Top, the showroom with its distinctive ware.

The Cob Cottage Pottery which is run by Royce and Trudi McGlashen is situated in the small town of Brightwater on the Waimea Plains 20 kilometres from Nelson.

The pottery features its own showroom and this is the only place in the province where its wares may be seen and purchased.

Royce is a qualified master potter having completed his apprenticeship at the Waimea Pottery. Royce travelled overseas to extend his experience and this included a visit to Bolivia and Peru in South America where he looked at ceramics and weaving.

Royce is a prolific producer and exhibitor.

Since 1980 he has conducted two one-week residential pottery schools each year at his workshop.

At present there are two potters working with him mostly on domestic wear such as casseroles, mugs, teapots, jugs, plates and goblets etc. About 30% of production consists of individual decorative and semi-sculptural pieces in both porcelain and stoneware. There are also tiles for panels for interior decoration and these are noted for Royce's beautiful brushwork decoration.

Top, Royce with an example of his work.

Above, the display gallery and workshop.

The recently modernised Suter Gallery incorporating as it does a large restaurant, a shop and all the necessary facilities for films, recitals and theatrical productions is arguably the most progressive to date of the New Zealand art galleries. More of an arts centre than a traditional art gallery, most of the areas within the gallery have been designed to be multifunctional and although its main purpose remains the care and display of works of art, its programme of other activities ensures a day to day throughput of nearly 90,000 visitors a year which is unusual even for much larger communities than Nelson.

The gallery sets out to beguile and entertain but never overtly to educate. The restaurant with its large balcony overlooking Queen's Gardens is open at all times that the gallery is open, and provides good food and an elegant setting in which to contemplate and relax.

The Suter Gallery's high national reputation is due in no small measure to its overall philosophy that galleries should primarily be for people and that the first consideration must be an environment which people enjoy.

Top left, the gallery's popular restaurant.
Left, an art exhibition.
Above, a display of ceramics.

It has been said that Copperfield's is the finest independent giftware shop in New Zealand. Certainly few would disagree that with its interesting and varied stock, set off by original and imaginative window displays, Copperfield's has become one of the institutions of Nelson.

Established in 1979 by Lance and Michael Edwardes, the concept behind Copperfield's was to maintain a high quality of service and to create an atmosphere where both Nelsonians and holidaymakers could browse at leisure.

Originally coming to the area on a working holiday to pick tobacco in Riwaka, Michael, like many before him, became enchanted by the area's natural beauty. He returned to settle after living and working in Canada for six years. Lance came to the district to take up a teaching post after completing an honours degree in the UK. Together they settled upon Bridge Street as the place in which to test their ideas.

Like many successful stores, Copperfield's is based upon the premise that shopping, which so often is a chore, should instead be a pleasant and entertaining social outing.

Building upon the successful ideas behind Copperfield's is the Company Reserve, the latest venture (still under development) by Michael and Lance Edwardes. It is planned as three separate shops linked by a walk through. The Hardy Street/Buxton Square location was chosen after much consideration as the site offering the most flexibility and the potential in which to create a lunch counter and shops where people could browse and also enjoy lunch or a coffee.

This interesting site, originally reserved by the Nelson Company in pioneering days, from which it derives its name, features a coin operated pianola and the proprietors hope to employ local artists to perform in the courtyard to entertain shoppers having lunch on those lovely sunny Nelson days.

Facing page: Top, an exterior view at night.
Mid right, an interior view showing the crystal stand.
Bottom right, an alternative interior view.

Top, the attractive exterior decoration.
Mid left, interior view.
Lower left, a window display during the day.
Bottom left, another attractive window display.

The Tahuna Beach Holiday Park is one of the most famous in New Zealand. It is also the biggest, having an occupancy rate of 480 people per night during the year—a phenomenal total of 175,000 bed nights annually.

The camp is famous not only for its size and its proximity to the renowned Tahuna Beach, but also for its services and facilities as well as for the variety of accommodation being offered.

The park occupies 20.5 hectares providing space for 1,200 tent and caravan sites which are served by six amenities blocks with kitchens, bathrooms and toilets. There is a large children's play area featuring a crazy golf course, trampolines, t.v. lounge, car wash and a large

camp store. The Nelson Golf Club course is next to the camp.

There is a tourist lodge complex in the camp. It has 37 units and there are 14 tourist flats with their own toilet facilities. Additionally there are two fully self contained motel units equipped for paraplegic use. These were constructed by the Nelson Lions Club for the New Zealand Crippled Children's Society.

It is the policy of the board administering the camp to provide low cost tariffs and to administer the camp for the benefit of its guests. To this effect an exemplary standard of behaviour is required and no noisy element is tolerated. During the Christmas holiday period the camp is

under night patrol until dawn.

The camp is non-profit making, all receipts going back into camp improvements.

Facing page: Left, an aerial view showing part of the beach looking towards Fifeshire Rock and Port Nelson.

Top right, caravan park.

Mid right, one of the tourist flats.

Bottom right, camp administration block.

Top left, part of the camping ground.

Mid left, kitchen facilities.

Bottom left, the main office.

Above, a view of the camp from the air.

Nelson offers a great deal of visitor accommodation but one of the most popular stopping places is the Trailways Motor Inn, situated by the Maitai River in Trafalgar Street at the opposite end to the cathedral.

A feature of the motor inn is its restaurant which is popular with the locals—always a good recommendation.

The accommodation is spacious and well decorated. Each room has a full range of facilities such as bathroom, television, radio and telephone, tea and coffee making facilities, refrigerator and laundry on the premises and all this right on Nelson's main street.

A well-stocked cocktail bar offers a wide range of New Zealand and imported ales and spirits—ideal after your walk around the main city shopping area.

The Trailways Motor Inn has 42 fully serviced units and three family suites with kitchenettes.

It is noted for its courteous and prompt service.

Trailways Motor Inn.
Top, the motor inn at night across the Maitai River.
Above, a view of the main restaurant.
Bottom right, an interior view of the popular bar at night.

Nelson has the distinction of having the oldest building society in New Zealand. The Permanent Building Society of Nelson was established in 1862 and has continued to grow strongly ever since. As a consequence many thousands of Nelsonians have been able to have their own homes.

In 1981 the name of the society was changed to the Nelson Building Society and the following year an NCR 9020 computer was installed and commissioned. Members can now visually observe their transactions being keyed on a video display unit at the counter and if these are correct, approve entry which passes to the account instantly. At the same time a separate printer records the transaction in the member's passbook and updates the account balance. Calculation of interest on members' accounts, which once would have taken a week's work on the ten thousand accounts, is accomplished in half an hour each day by the computer.

Most people know that the role of the Nelson Building Society remains unchanged—the provision of loans for home purchase. What has changed, however, is customer service and facilities. These have been redesigned and rebuilt by Berkett and West in the society's permanent premises in Trafalgar Street. Despite its new image, the society remains very much a home town institution owned, managed and operated by the people of Nelson for the people of Nelson and taking a full part in the community through the sponsorship of various sporting and social events.

Left, the society's premises.

Below, the redesigned interior gives customers quick and efficient service.

Top, one of the most popular attractions in the Nelson Province is Isel House, park and the Provincial Museum at Stoke. The park is acknowledged as one of the best examples of its kind and the house is a historic gem.

Mid right, the Provincial Museum is the repository of several outstanding photographic collections—the monochrome plates in this volume are from the museum—an attractive display of Nelson's colonial history and an outstanding display of Maori artifacts and pre-colonial material culture.

Bottom right, one of the churches of the Waimea.

Top left, Fairfield House.
Top right, Melrose House.
Left, Bishopdale.
Below, Broadgreen at Stoke.

The Rutherford Hotel honours the name of one of New Zealand's most distinguished sons.

Lord Rutherford was born and educated in Nelson before leaving for overseas and the pursuit of a brilliant academic career which led to the splitting of the atom and the recognition of his work through the award of the Nobel Prize and his elevation to the peerage.

The Rutherford Hotel is sited in the centre of the city within easy walking distance of the main shopping area. It is an imposing building and features many of the amenities and facilities of a top international hotel. It is a favourite of visiting tourists and businessmen, and is very much in demand as a convention centre.

It is a popular rendezvous for Nelsonians as well.

Facing page: the Rutherford Hotel at night.

Top, the main entrance and reception lobby.
Above, the hotel offers a number of suites with a separate lounge area.
Above right, one of the spacious bedrooms.

The Bank of New Zealand is one of the oldest business enterprises in Nelson. Apart from its historic significance, the bank plays an important part in the economy of the province, both as a commercial enterprise and as a substantial employer. More than 90 people work in the various branches of the bank throughout the province.

The BNZ is wholly New Zealand owned—a singular distinction as it is the only one without overseas interests. It was incorporated in 1861 and the next year a branch was opened in Nelson in Hardy Street and four years later moved to its present site, though the original building was replaced by the present premises in 1970.

The bank provides the full range of banking services such as cheque and savings accounts, higher interest accounts, BNZ Visa credit cards, loans, international travel, automatic teller machines. These and many more services are supported by an on-line national computer network.

Top, the BNZ premises in Trafalgar Street.
Above, an interior view of the spacious premises.

Top left, Roly, Cathy and children at the main entrance.
Top right, an exterior view of the charming cottage.
Above, an interior view.

Roly Taylor wanted to be a chef so instead his father made him become a carpenter. Roly lost the battle but his father lost the war—Roly is now chef and in partnership with his wife also the proprietor of the Coachlamps Restaurant.

Roly's final triumph owes much to his wife Cathy who supported his ambition because that is also what she wanted. Now they work together providing the meals that their establishment has made famous.

At the time they met Roly was managing a roofing and building business in Christchurch. Soon after they were married they embarked on an extensive overseas tour which confirmed their desire to have their own intimate restaurant.

But despite their intention, this was not to happen immediately they returned home from Europe. Roly resumed his old trade on his own account. He began restoring old houses before accepting a contract to build two large glasshouses in Papua New Guinea. They next went to Ballarat in Australia where he built the two largest known glasshouses in the world.

Coachlamps they say is all they have ever dreamed of. Roly renovated and decorated the building to give it its unique charm. You feel as if you could be in a small cafe in France or Greece.

Roly and Cathy and their daughters Kersha and Annalese plan more overseas travel to learn as much as possible of the various aspects of food preparation in the countries they will visit.

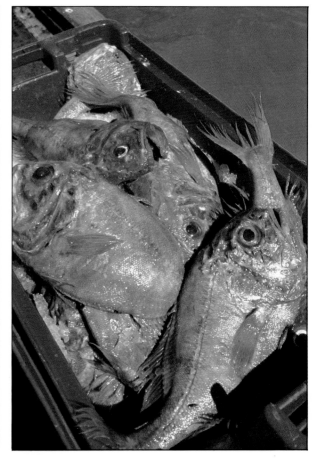

An indication of the important role played by fisheries in Nelson's economy is demonstrated by the fact that Sealord Products has the largest processing plant in Australasia and that with 650 staff is the single biggest employer in the Nelson Province.

The plant occupies 4 ha of land at Port Nelson where its own ships and those of share fishermen discharged 45,000 tonnes of fish last year. The plant processed 25,000 tonnes and the balance was exported whole.

The annual wage bill is nearly $10 million and many million more are spent with local companies for material and services.

The annual turnover is $50 million of which $42 million represents export sales, mostly shipped through the Port of Nelson to Australia, Japan, U S A, Saudi Arabia and other destinations.

Facing page, the company's flagship, mv *Arrow* on her way to the fishing grounds.

Top left, at sea on the fishing grounds with preparation of the trawling net nearly complete.

Above, orange roughy, a close view of New Zealand's latest sea delicacy.

Left, the catch is hauled in.

Sealord is a value-added processor—the company philosophy is to add value to the natural resource. Range of products produced include: wet fish—fillets, headed and gutted, whole; breaded products—fish fingers, dinner cuts; battered fish products; fish with sauce products—cook in bag, oven tray; canned fish from the company's cannery; by-products such as fishmeal and fish oil; and canned abalone.

Sealord has its own fleet of fishing vessels—four trawlers, the largest being the 51 metre, 550 ton *Arrow*. These are known as "freshers" with the catch packed in ice at sea and landed whole at the factory in Nelson for processing.

The company operates a purse seiner, the *Shemara* which fishes for pelagic (surface swimming) fish such as kahawai and mackerel. This catch is also landed fresh and is destined mainly for canning.

Sealord also deploys charter vessels from its Japanese partners. These are much larger than the domestic vessels, up to 2,500 tons. These are freezer trawlers, i.e. they partly process the catch at sea in headed and gutted form, and freeze it. They can stay at sea for two or three months at a time.

Sealord holds quota under the Government Deep Water Policy and has been allocated 31,382 tonnes of the prime deep water species out of the total quota of 167,050 tonnes. These prime species include barracouta, hake, hoki, ling, orange roughy, oreo dory, silver warehou and squid.

Facing page: Top left, pelagic fish discharged from the mv *Shemarra* with a vacuum pump.

Above left, Sealord processing plant on 4 ha at Port Nelson.

Inset, the General Manager of Sealord, Mr G U France.

Top right, an interior view of the factory.

Above, orange roughy about to go through the processing machine.

A vital role in the development of overseas markets for Nelson's expanding horticultural and fisheries products is being played by TNL Export Ltd, part of the TNL Group of companies, one of the oldest in the province.

Transport Nelson began its life by providing badly needed transport in the newly established colony. It grew with the province and later, with the country. It is now one of New Zealand's major companies.

Nelson's superb climate is ideal for the production of exceptional quality berry fruit and pip fruit for which there is an increasing demand throughout the world.

Boysenberries, black currants, strawberries are exported, and recently kiwifruit has joined the export list as the crop has begun to mature in the province.

Exports now amount to more than $8 million and this includes the latest New Zealand food sensation to be presented to the world: KiwiClams. These are the unique green mussel which thrives in the clean waters of the Sounds.

TNL Export has recognised the need to develop overseas markets for New Zealand's abundant horticultural and fisheries products and especially from its home province of Nelson where the company's headquarters are still situated.

Above, strawberries being harvested for export (*Trevor Hyde & Paul E Dixon*).

Facing page: TNL's rising star, KiwiClams, marketed with great success in Japan, Australia and the United States (*Trevor Hyde & Paul E Dixon*).

The freighting division of Transport Nelson is one of the major companies of the province. It employs 440 people in the Nelson area and 349 others throughout New Zealand.

The company was formed in 1938 by the amalgamation of several local carriers. Its objective was to provide the Nelson region with a thoroughly professional transportation system. Mr Putt Boyes became its manager and Sir Jack Newman was appointed Chairman of Directors.

The new company set up in Hardy Street and continued growing until the outbreak of the war when several executives were seconded to the army.

After the war Transport Nelson introduced truck and trailer concepts to road transport in New Zealand and continued to grow until November 1952 when shares were listed on the stock exchange and the company became open to the public. In the 1960s the company diversified by adding civil contracting to its list of services and moved to Port Nelson as the Hardy Street premises now were inadequate. The controversial closure of the Nelson rail branch line gave the company the added responsibility of linking with the railhead in Blenheim.

In 1973 Newmans was amalgamated with Transport Nelson Holdings Ltd and in 1977 the TNL Group Ltd was formed.

Top, close view of Nelson's export delicacy—the boysenberry (*Trevor Hyde & Paul E Dixon*).

Above, boysenberries under machine harvest (*Trevor Hyde & Paul E Dixon*).

Above, One of Transport Nelson's latest trucks in its new colours at the depot at Port Nelson.

A family business which started life as Berko Products in 1958 producing farm gates, building milking sheds and hay barns is now Berkett Construction, one of the major companies in the Nelson area with impressive credits to its name.

The company which employs 40 staff is guided by its founder, Murray Berkett, working shareholders and key personnel. It is engaged in a wide range of building projects from concept to completion.

The company has attracted stable staff with a wide range of skills in the construction industry.

The company specialised in steel work and prestressed concrete, skills that gave it a competitive edge.

Berkett Construction was quick to realise that the provision of an architect and an engineer to discuss client needs would give it an extra edge and employed architect Greg West and engineer Hans Dukker.

Top, TNL House was an earlier Berkett Construction project and is a recognised Nelson point of interest.

Above, the Marble Arch complex is one of Nelson's landmarks. It was built by Berkett Construction using the skills of Greg West and Hans Dukker.

Nelson's Bridge Street is one of its major commercial centres and Bishops Jewellers are easily distinguished from the other shop frontages because of its Takaka marble facing and entry and two inner pillars that have been tiled inside the shop.

The store is a second generation family business which was established in 1940 by Mr Eric E Bishop. Except for during the war it has been in constant operation since.

At present the business is run by Jim and Wendy Bishop who share the belief that only genuine items will be offered for sale.

The visitor will be interested to know that there is a large selection of New Zealand made jewellery as well as a wide range of items from New Zealand nephrite jade and paua shell.

There is also an extensive range of Japanese watches as well as clocks, silverware, crystals and trophies.

Top left, the entrance showing the use of Takaka marble.
Left, Jim and Wendy Bishop.
Below, an interior view.

In 1857 Nathaniel Edwards and Company set up a small foundry in Nelson and thus began the first step of what has become a major business enterprise known today as Anchor-Dorman.

In 1870 the name "Anchor" came into being with the setting up of a shipping service and in 1880 the company became known as the Anchor Shipping and Foundry Company Limited. In 1969 Anchor purchased T Dorman Engineering and the company became known by its present name.

In 1982 the Anchor Shipping division became the Nelson branch of the Union Shipping Group Ltd., operating under Union Maritime Services Ltd.

Anchor-Dorman plays an important role in the economy of Nelson through the employment of more than 100 skilled men and the provision of important facilities and services which attract important industry to Nelson.

Work handled by the company includes all types of plant installation, design and construction of purpose-made machinery, ships and boats of all kinds, mechanical handling plant, logging equipment, road transport truck bodies and the execution of its own innovative designs, such as the "conporter".

Top, *Tangaroa*, a trader used on the Cook Islands circuit, in dry dock.

Above, a general view of the workshop.

Facing page: A huge ship's propeller at the Anchor-Dorman workshop.

Above, one of the highly successful "Conporters" designed and built at Nelson.

Mid right, Anchor-Dorman survey, service and outfit visiting ships as well as acting as agents for Russian trawlers.

Bottom right, arranging a lift of equipment at Port Nelson.

The development of the Nelson Province over the past 140 years has depended heavily on its port and the shipping services, both coastal and overseas, that have contributed much to the growth and prosperity of the district.

Union Maritime Services Limited is a division of the Union Shipping Group which has been trading through the Port of Nelson for over a century. The company provides a regular roll on roll-off service for trans-Tasman trade with mv *Union Sydney* and mv *Union Dunedin* to Sydney and Melbourne with trans-shipment services to other Australian Ports.

Mv *Union Nelson* is the latest in a long history of vessels which have served Nelson in the coastal trade to Onehunga. This trade was formerly served by vessels of the Anchor Shipping and Foundry Co Ltd which had been in the business of coastal shipping out of Nelson since 1862.

Union Stevedoring Services Limited was formed in 1981 as a partnership between Nelson Stevedores Limited and Union Maritime Services Limited.

This new company has the benefit of personnel with a depth of experience in the stevedoring field covering many years and a wide variety of cargoes ranging through export fruit for the New Zealand Apple and Pear Board to Europe, North America, South East Asia and the Middle East, frozen fish and squid to Japan, South East Asia and USSR: kiwifruit to North America and Japan, gypsum from Australia, Honda car parts from Japan and a variety of other shipments through the busy Port of Nelson.

This page: *Union Nelson* discharging at Port Nelson.

Fashion, footwear and flowers—this is the story of an interesting Nelson company which began its life selling fashionwear and has grown to include a clothes factory employing eighty staff, a shoe shop and a vast complex of glasshouses growing orchids for export.

The company was founded by Mr and Mrs Graham Fergusson in 1962 when they opened a retail business in Bridge Street and named it The Miss Nelson. In the early years Graham Fergusson sent samples of overseas fashions to a small factory called Martha Washington. These were copied and became best sellers making him realise that what sold for him in Nelson would sell throughout New Zealand. Graham bought a share in the factory and launched the brand Suzy Speed which has since become a leading brand name nationwide.

Today the second generation Fergusson family run the factory and The Miss Nelson shop. Two doors up Bridge Street is the oldest shoe store in New Zealand and this has been added to the company to offer a complete fashion service. It is now possible to outfit at The Miss Nelson with the latest fashion wear from either the Suzy Speed range or other top New Zealand labels and to move up the street to Healey's Shoes and complement the selection with a choice of the latest footwear.

The latest addition to the Suzy Speed Holdings has been a row of glasshouses in Stoke where tens of thousands of cymbidium orchid plants are grown in the very latest greenhouse technology under the brand name of Kiwi Orchids for export to Europe, Japan and America.

Top right, one of the glasshouses full or orchids for export.
Mid right, the Martha Washington Clothes Factory.
Bottom right, an interior view of The Miss Nelson Fashionware Shop.

Facing page: Bottom, an exterior view of Healey's Shoes.

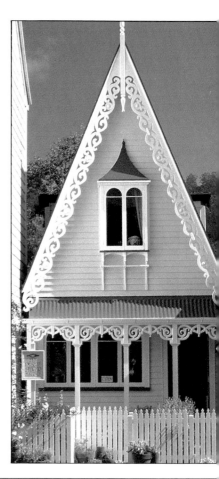

Views of Nelson houses—old and new.

Robinson Brothers is an orchard and winery at Stoke with a fascinating history. It is a story of remarkable endeavour. The original orchard was established by Thomas Robinson in 1910 when he was 65 years old. Six years later at the age of 71 Thomas married Susan Stephenson and started a family. Thomas died at the age of 91, leaving his wife and four children.

Susan ran the orchard, which she named Ardilea after her father's home in Ireland, until the boys were old enough to take over.

The company is now run by Thomas and his son Colin and is a popular stopping place among the people of Nelson who go there to get their supply of natural juices, table fruit, wines (both fruit and grape) and ciders, including a sparkling cider Ardilea named in honour of Thomas senior and his wife Susan.

The property is clearly signposted on the main road south and there is ample parking for visitors who are encouraged to come and sample the juices and wines.

Top right, father and son carrying on the tradition—Colin, left, Thomas on the right.

Mid right, the season's first apples, Gravensteins, being harvested.

Bottom right, the giant Swiss juice press which gives Robinsons pure, unadulterated juice.

Below, portrait of Thomas senior who started the orchard when he was 65 years old.

The Arthur Wakefield Restaurant in Richmond is regarded as one of Nelson's top dining-out venues. It was established by Anthony and Marion Smith in 1979 following an extensive search for a suitable building in a suitable location.

The restaurant is named after Captain Arthur Wakefield, brother of Edward Gibbon Wakefield, one of the founders of the New Zealand Company which was responsible for the settlement of Nelson in 1842.

The decor reflects the stately charm of days gone by in a building from the 1890s which has been tastefully restored to its former glory.

The menu offers an extensive selection with an emphasis on steak and seafood. There is an ample choice of wine from the cellar.

A feature of the restaurant is the use of pottery carafes and goblets made by Jane Gregory and beer steins by Justin Gardner.

Top, the main dining room.
Mid left, an exterior view.
Left, mine host Anthony Smith at the bar.

Top, a general view of Stoke showing the estuary and the mountains.
Bottom, close view of Stoke with Broadgreen in the centre.

Above, John Walker winning the Molenberg Mile in Trafalgar Street.

The Molenberg Mile won this year in Nelson in a final sprint up Trafalgar Street by John Walker is now a recognised annual event in the country's sporting calendar.

What few people realise, however, is that Quality Bakers NZ Limited which sponsor the top athletes from around the world to compete in the series of races, is based in Nelson and very much part of the Nelson province through the Goodman Black Haycock Bakeries Ltd whose Homestyle bread is delivered from Whangamoa to Murchison and Collingwood.

The bread is produced in 38 styles of loaves in a modern bakery in Bolt Road where about 4,680,000 loaves are baked each year.

The company also produces pastry under the Bellamys brand and this is distributed throughout New Zealand.

Facing page: Bottom left, loaves by the mile—some of the 4,680,000 loaves on the production line.

Left, the loaves on the conveyor for automatic wrapping.

Below, the sales and administration staff at the company's new bakery.

Bottom, pastry being manufactured.

Boasting an excellent record of industrial relations is one of the area's largest employers, NZMC Ltd's vehicle assembly plant in Stoke, which assembles the unique commuter Honda City, the up-market Honda Accord range and the rugged four-wheel drive Land Rover.

Set up in 1965 in the harmony of a rural atmosphere, the modern 13,000 square metre plant provides a living for approximately 340 Nelsonians, who place a high emphasis on productivity and quality assurance.

These people currently build some 7,000 vehicles a year, thus contributing to more than 45 per cent of NZMC Ltd's combined annual sales turnover.

NZMC Ltd, the largest subsidiary company of the Wellington based EMCO Group Ltd, has another car assembly plant in Auckland and 88 sales outlets throughout New Zealand. Eighteen outlets belong to the company and trade under the name of Motorcorp.

In Nelson the company has always enjoyed a special relationship with the local community, which has lead to an ongoing policy of sourcing compentry wherever possible in the area. Over the years substantial contracts have been awarded to several local suppliers.

Since it began operation in the sixties, the plant has assembled a range of Leyland, Triumph, Jaguar, Daimler and Rover cars. During the 1970's a substantial number of eight cylinder Rovers were exported to Australia.

Until 1982 the plant also built a range of British Leyland commercial vehicles such as the Leyland A.E.C., Albion and Scammel. These include passenger vehicles like the Bristol Bell bus, which today forms a substantial part of the Christchurch Transport Board's fleet of public passenger vehicles.

The plant began building Land Rover and its many variants in the mid seventies and still continues to do so today.

The most significant change in the history of the plant occurred in 1980 with the transition from British Leyland to the assembly of Honda cars. Japanese car now form more than 90 per cent of the plant's production.

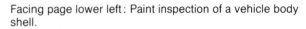

Facing page lower left: Paint inspection of a vehicle body shell.

Top left: The trim assembly line prior to fitting engines and road running gear.

Bottom left: In the foreground, NZMC Ltd's plant at Stoke.

Top right: The plant's extensive engineering maintenance workshop.

Above: Finishing Land Rover chassis weld.

The Waitaki New Zealand Refrigerating works at Stoke has enjoyed considerable publicity for the proving of the latest technology in the industry. The machine in question is an automatic pelting device which was shown to be successful at the Stoke works and has thus opened the way for its acceptance by the rest of the meat works throughout New Zealand.

The plant is of critical importance to Nelson's economic prosperity. This is not only because it employs 300 people on a full-time basis throughout the year and contributes $6 million in wages, but also because it services the farming community from Golden Bay, Motueka, Nelson, Murchison, Springs Junction, Reefton and Westport areas.

The money spent on purchase of stock is also put back in the local economy.

The Stoke works is considered small by national standards, but it is regarded as one of the most efficient. It enjoys a stable, loyal and conscientious work force. There are few industrial, absentee or injury problems at Stoke, which are commonly associated with the meat industry.

The plant runs one sheep and lamb chain processing 3,200 units per day (approximately 400,000 a year).

It has one beef chain killing and boning 192 cattle per day (approximately 30,000 a year).

Bobby calves are processed over the winter months on the mutton chain. Some 25,000 are killed each season.

The plant meets the latest hygiene requirements and also provides "Halal" slaughtermen for animals killed for Muslim markets.

Top right, an aerial view of the Stoke works.
Bottom right, lamb carcasses coming through the pelting machine pioneered at the works.

Facing page: Bottom left, on the mutton chain.
Bottom right, the beef boning room.

It is easy to take electricity for granted and hard to appreciate how difficult it is to reticulate it over an area of some 10,000 square kilometres. Yet this is a job done with distinction by the Tasman Electric Power Board.

Some of the difficulties faced by the Board are well illustrated by the Farewell Spit light. This is a vital beacon to navigation and to make sure it continues to shine, the Tasman Electric Power Board has put in the longest underground cable from Puponga to the end of the spit where the lighthouse stands, a distance of some 27 kilometres.

Few people in the province would realise that the board is a large modern corporation playing an important part in the local economy by providing employment for some 200 people and having a turnover of $22,000,000 each year.

The board has a permanent administration headed by Mr J C Rogers who implement policy laid down by 12 board members, elected every three years by the public.

As well as the reticulation of electricity, the board operates five retail outlets specialising in electrical appliances. These are located at Richmond, where the board's head office is situated, Nelson, Motueka, Takaka and Murchison.

Facing page: Top, problems of power reticulation are demonstrated by Farewell Spit—the board dug 27 km of trench for a power cable.

Mid right, the General Manager, Mr Rogers, in his office.

Above, the board's head office and showroom at Richmond.

Mid left, design and drafting offices at Richmond.

Bottom left, display of goods at the Richmond showroom.

99

The area administered by the Richmond Borough Council is the most important to the continued development of Nelson because of its urban industrial potential. In other words, Nelson and Stoke have run out of land but Richmond has plenty.

The borough dates from 1842 when it was surveyed for settlement. In 1866 it was proclaimed a town district and in 1891 it was constituted a borough.

The township is at the head of the fertile Waimea plains and acts both as a residential area for Nelson and a service centre for the rural hinterland. The demand for additional residential land and industrial space will continue to make Richmond ever more important in the economy of the province.

The borough is well-prepared for its future role. It has excellent educational facilities with Waimea College being regarded as a top secondary school in New Zealand and a complex of other schools with common borders with the college—an intermediate school, two primary schools and a special school for girls.

There is a race course and showgrounds, library, the Washbourne Gardens, a country club, Y M C A and various other facilities.

Facing page: Bottom left, an aerial view of the borough looking towards the estuary.

Top right, a magnificent display at the begonia house at the Washbourne Gardens.

Mid right, a close up view of the main shopping area.

Bottom right, a view of one of the new subdivisions.

Top left, lunchtime at the Waimea Intermediate School.

Bottom left, a residence for senior citizens.

Above, the rich, fertile Waimea Plains adjoining the borough.

The Cawthron Institute is a unique Nelson institution and one of New Zealand's oldest scientific research centres. It was established immediately after World War 1 under a bequest from the estate of a Nelson trader and investor, Thomas Cawthron. It was subsequently given statutory permanence by Parliament under the Thomas Cawthron Trust Act 1924.

The Cawthron, as it is known locally, is devoted to basic research on microbes and to providing confidential industrial testing for the private and public sectors, feasibility studies, and social and environmental consultancy services.

The institute has a staff of 50, more than half of whom are employed in commercial activities including research into intertidal sediments and advising on natural resources development in Asia, the Pacific and Central America.

The institute is governed by a board of 10 members, comprising local public office holders and representatives appointed by the Governor General and the Minister of Science.

Facing page: The Waimea estuary has been the basis of much of the institute's experiments.

Above, competent scientists are the basis for the institute's success. A group photograph with the principals seated in the front row. They are from left to right: R. Lason, administration officer; Dr R.H. Thornton, Director; A. Cooke, Manager, technical services and Dr P. Gillespie.

Left, the institute's modern office and laboratory blocks in Nelson.

The present Baigent Company has grown from a family sawmilling business established at Wakefield in 1843 by Edward Baigent. H Baigent & Sons Ltd was established in the early 1930s and was initially engaged in milling indigenous timber at a number of small mills in Waimea, Marlborough, Golden Bay and Buller counties.

The supply of native logs was clearly limited so the company began to purchase radiata pine woodlots to ensure its future log supplies. In 1945 the company started large-scale afforestation. Land holdings now total nearly 26,000 ha mainly in Waimea County. 18,500 ha under exotic forest (almost 100% radiata pine) and new planting continues at an annual rate of 400 ha.

The company's forests have been planted mostly on scrubland, reverted hill pasture or abandoned orchard land. They are concentrated in the northern half of Waimea County between the Motueka and Wai-iti Rivers, but with a significant area in the Eastern Hills and outliers near Riwaka and in the Pearse and Slippery valleys.

The company raises its own seedlings in the forest nursery at Spring Grove and by 1988 will be self-supporting in the production of genetically improved radiata pine seed from its orchard in Brightwater.

The company exotic forests have been in full production for 10 years and annually yield about 200,000 cubic metres of logs. Currently 65% of the latter are sawn to timber in company mills at Harakeke, Brookside and Wakefield or are exported to Japan and Korea in log form. The balance is exported as pulpwood or as chips or is processed through the treated post/pole yard at Brookside. Sawmill slabs are also chipped.

Most of the forest area which is logged each year (about 500 ha) reseeds itself naturally to establish a new crop. The latter is then selectively thinned to remove undesirable and surplus trees. Eventually, all logged forest will be replaced and all new plantings will be made with select nursery seedling raised from orchard seed.

Top, chip and log stockpiles at Port Nelson awaiting export to Japan. The darker coloured chips are produced by Nelson Pine Forests Ltd from native beech species. The light coloured chips are largely processed from radiata pine and are produced mainly by H. Baigent & Sons Ltd.

Mid right, packs of radiata pine timber arriving at Port Nelson for export to Australia.

Bottom right, pressure treating packs of radiata pine timber with "Tanalith" salts to prevent fungal decay and insect attack.

Facing page: Loading logs for export at Port Nelson

Approximately 140 men are employed full time in company forests on seed collection, nursery work, planting, tending, road construction and logging. A further 240 staff are employed in the company's other operations, principally in the various production plants.

Baigents are developing a major new forestry complex at Eves Valley, approximately 25 km southwest of Nelson. The objective is to centralise all of the company's production activities on one site and for Eves Valley to be the location of all future development of the company's production. At the same time, it is intended to incorporate the most modern technology into the production processes to ensure that the company's product is of a standard and price competitive on the major export markets.

The initial development, which commenced in 1983 involves the establishment of a new sawmill with the associated timber processing facilities at a cost in excess of $30 million. This complex will replace the company's existing sawmills at Brookside, Wakefield and Harakeke, and the timber processing facilities at Stoke and Nelson. It will almost treble the sawn timber output of the company to 82,500 cubic metres per year as well as chipping the mill and forest residue.

Facing page: Top left, sowing radiata pine seed in the company's forest nursery at Spring Grove. Seed is usually sown in October and the resultant seedlings are ready for planting out in the forest by June of the following year.

Centre right, contractors thinning natural regeneration.

Mid right, part of Baigents' 18 500 hectare man-made forest. Looking westwards from above the head of Eves Valley.

Bottom right, radiata pine seedlings, 8 months old, ready for planting in the forest. Spring Grove nursery.

Left, loading logs north of Pigeon Valley.

Above, log transport. A company "Kenworth" in the Roding Valley.

Site construction commenced in January 1984 and this first stage of the Eves Valley Development is planned to be in operation by September 1985.

The mill will rely primarily on Baigent forests for its log supply. The company will also continue to purchase logs from other forest owners in the Nelson district including the NZ Forest Service. The sawmill will initially operate on one shift, but will be expanded into a two-shift operation as increased quantities of logs become available. A major increase in the log production of the Nelson district will occur from about 1990. Those volumes are expected to be sufficient for the establishment of an integrated major pulp and

paper complex in Eves Valley. This expansion could provide employment for in excess of a thousand people and will increase Nelson's forestry-related export earnings by in excess of $100 million per year.

A vital role in Nelson's communications with the rest of New Zealand is played by Air New Zealand and judging by the numbers of people travelling, such a service is essential.

Air New Zealand has nine daily flights to Nelson and these are from and to Auckland, Wellington and Christchurch, including a direct link with Auckland, and from these main centres to other parts of the country.

Some 230 passengers use the service each day—approximately 84,800 each year.

The airport and the attractive terminal are sited within a short distance of the centre of the city.

Top, one of Air New Zealand's Friendships outside the terminal.

This page: Views from the air of the Waimea Plains.

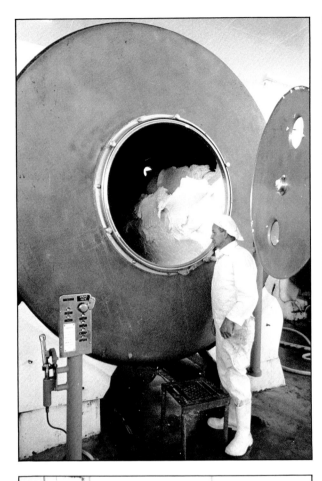

The Waimea Co-operative Dairy Company plays an important role in the economy of the Nelson Province. It is the mainstay of the 68 suppliers who farm throughout the Waimea, Tapawera, Murchison and Springs Junction areas.

The factory is situated at Brightwater and is South Island's pioneer in the installation of a woodwaste energy conservation unit for all the company's boiler requirements. The distinct silver smokestack is a landmark.

The unit burns sawdust, chips and bark and has saved the company large sums of money that

would normally be spent on fuel oil.

The company employs 23 staff at the factory and three others at Murchison in a trading store.

The company's suppliers and the Nelson Milk Producers Association produce raw material for 1,500 tonnes of creamery butter, 2,400 tonnes of skim and buttermilk powder and 110 tonnes of whey butter each year.

Butter produced at the factory is used in the Nelson–Marlborough area and as far south as Kaikoura. Spray milk powder is both for domestic and overseas markets.

Facing page, top: This is a conventional butter churn that is currently being used. However, the company is commissioning a continuous butter making machine that is a totally enclosed proven process.

Bottom, the Van-De-Ploog Quadruple Effect Evaporator that makes concentrate for milk powder drying and is sufficiently versatile to make concentrate of fruit juices and other products that require long-life keeping qualities.

Above, this aerial photograph shows the factory complex and part of the township of Brightwater.

Two townships of the Waimea Plains. Top, an aerial view of Wakefield.   Above, an aerial view of Brightwater.

The kiwifruit boom in the Nelson district has given added impetus to a long established Nelson fruit wine maker who now produces a kiwifruit wine that has been highly praised for its quality.

Redwood Cellars Ltd situated in Redwoods Valley (30 minutes from Nelson) have used experience gained from many years of fruit wine production — principally apple wines, apple ciders and boysenberry wine, to produce a highly successful kiwifruit wine that has been compared with the best light riesling wines.

The winery currently produces two types of kiwifruit wine, both named after historic houses

Above, Redwood cellars Kiwifruit vintage displayed to advantage at Hoddy's orchard between Hope and Brightwater.

of the province. These houses constructed over 100 years ago feature as background sketches on the wine labels.

Redwood Cellars fruit winery was established to process some of the surplus quantities of apples from the province and it now is able to adapt its technology and experience to absorb surplus quantities of kiwifruit that fail to meet the export season.

It seems appropriate that two former school teachers should run a restaurant which is a converted school house. This is exactly what has happened to Karen and Bill Hamlen-Williams at Mapua.

Karen and Bill and their son David arrived at Mapua in 1980 seeking an alternative life-style. Part of their philosophy was to provide an attractive dining out spot for locals and visitors as there was no restaurant outside Nelson and Motueka.

They established the Inlet restaurant from a 1930 school house which was brought out from Tasman Street, Nelson, and have made it the centre of much of Mapua's social life.

The restaurant specialises in light luncheons, afternoon teas and full evening meals. There is ample space for outdoor dining on the verandah and a cheerful warm atmosphere around the pot belly stove during the winter.

The restaurant features musical evenings each Thursday using local music groups. Craft fairs take place regularly every three weeks on Sundays.

Top, an aerial view of the Inlet, wharf and township.
Above, Bill and Karen with friends on the balcony.
Bottom left, an interior view of the restaurant.

Above, Buskers at the fair.
Below, a craft fair.

The Mapua Leisure Park is one of the most unusual motorcamps in the country. The park is the only optional resort in the country where visitors are free to take off all their clothes or to leave them on as they wish.

The park, which is set on approximately 10 ha of peninsula next to the Mapua Inlet, is covered with a mature stand of pine trees offering ample and delightful space for caravans and tents. Many of the sites have power points and there are two toilet and shower blocks; coffee bar, sports facilities such as tennis and mini tennis, a children's adventure playground with trampolines and table tennis.

There is a lovely beach with safe swimming regardless of the tide and this is a feature of the park.

The park was developed by Kathy Trott, her late husband and a group of investors some of whom take an active part in the management.

The park grew from the idea that there should be a family camping ground organised with activities and entertainment to make family holidays enjoyable.

There are also evening programmes and communal barbecues for the parents.

The camp is developing waterfront motor units and these can only add to the attractions offered by the park.

It is the only "alternative" camping ground in Australasia where naked people mingle with

those who are not prepared to take off all their clothes. The atmosphere is particularly relaxed and pleasant and attractive to those who have been curious but never brave enough to visit a nudist colony. At Mapua Leisure Park you can hedge your bets and enjoy the best of both worlds.

Facing page: Bottom, the beach.

Top left, caravans among trees.

Left, some of the shareholders. Left to right, Shirley and Murray Tuffery, Kathy Trott (Manager), David Hutton and Margaret and Neil Clark.

Top right and above, body painting.

Below, an aerial view of the bushclad peninsula.

Facing page: Top left, an aerial view at Mapua.
Left, farmhouses from the air.

Left, the bluffs of Ruby Bay.
Above, an aerial view of Tasman looking towards the Kina Peninsula and the Abel Tasman Park beyond.
Below, a well-known landmark at Ruby Bay.

Above, an aerial view of Upper Moutere with large plantations of hops below. The village of Upper Moutere is in the middle of the foreground.

Right, an aerial view of the extensive pine forests.

Lower right, a view from Harley Road.

Left, the annual Wine Festival.
Mid left, a view of the Motueka River.
Below, an aerial view of Motueka.

More than 140 years after an attempted settlement by a group of German migrants in the Moutere area, their original dream of growing grapes and making wines has been realised.

Two of the wineries are in Upper Moutere within 8 kilometres of each other and the other is at Ruby Bay. These are family run enterprises and they share one thing in common: a dedication to producing wines of excellent quality.

The wineries are Weingut Seifried; Neudorf and Korepo at Ruby Bay.

Of the three, the largest is Weingut Seifried run by the husband and wife partnership of Hermann and Agnes Seifried. It is also the oldest established.

Hermann is a graduate from a German wine institute. He came to New Zealand to work for the Apple and Pear Board to make fruit wines. He married a New Zealand girl and in 1973 decided to make wines on his own account and along the way has confirmed his judgement that excellent verital wines can be made in Nelson—a fact proved by the large sweep of medals their wines win at national competitions and festivals and the demand for their product. This year they brought home a gold medal for their late picked riesling and a silver for the gamay beaujolais from the Auckland Easter Show as well as many bronze medals, and the Cup for the champion wine by a South Island wine maker. The winery has an attractive roadside bottle shop where the wines may be sampled and purchased.

A short distance away, a little further down the Moutere Valley is the very attractive establishment of Neudorf Vineyards owned and operated by Tim and Judy Finn. This vineyard is named after the settlement established 140 years ago by German settlers from the Rhine. The vineyard has cabernet sauvigon, gewurztraminer, gamay de beaujolais, muller-thurgau, semillon, merlot and shiraz grapes have been planted and vinted. The winery is a popular stopping-place both for gate sales of wine and for the food served in an attractive setting and

atmosphere. Winners of silver medals last year and the Easter Show Cup for the champion wine by a South Island wine maker.

Korepo Wines was founded by Jane and Craig Gass in 1976 on a 4 hectare property at Ruby Bay. This small vineyard and winery, situated in a sheltered valley with its own micro-climate, has been planted out in some of the world's finest classical grape varieties, which include: chardonnay, rhine riesling, sauvignon blanc, pinot noir, gamay beaujolais, cabernet sauvignon and pinot meunier. From this range of grapes a selection of predominantly dry classical wines are made by time revered traditional wine making techniques. Since its first commercial production in 1980, Korepo Wines has consistently won medals for its wines at the National Wine competition.

Facing page: Top, a selection of prize winning wines at the Upper Moutere vineyard.
Mid right, Hermann and Agnes Seifried.
Bottom right, Tim and Judy Finn at their restaurant with a bottle of their prize-winning cabernet sauvignon wine.

Above, the attractive setting of the winery and restaurant.
Left, Craig and Jane Gass of Korepo Wines.
Below, the Korepo Vineyard sloping down towards Tasman Bay.

Above, clematis.
Right, kiwifruit, Riwaka.
Below, plum blossoms at Hope.

Facing page: Upper Motueka River Valley.

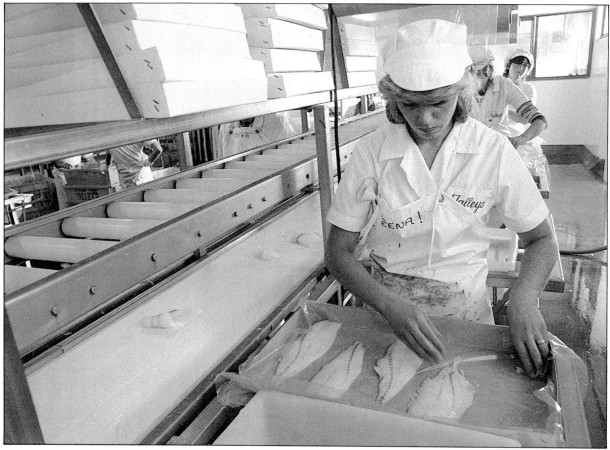

Talley's Fisheries is a family operated business which has grown spectacularly in recent years and has established itself as a vital factor in the economy of Motueka where its processing plant is situated.

A wide variety of inshore and deepwater fish species are handled and turned into an extensive range of products for local and overseas markets. A specialty is a line of marinated green mussels.

The plant is situated at Port Motueka and receives the fish at its own door as it comes off the boats, most of which are owner operated. The raw product is fully utilised with various by-products being manufactured and these include fishmeal, fertiliser and oil. Talley's have scored a notable success by being able to run their plant by using fish oil to fire the boilers.

Talley's now also plays an important role in the local horticulture industry by processing vegetables during the season. These are canned and frozen for both local and overseas markets.

Fish processing plants have also been established in Takaka, Westport and Greymouth.

Facing page: Select fillets being packed for export.

Left, Fish fillets on the processing line.
Mid left, Inside the fish processing shed with workers filleting orange roughy.
Below, A view of the plant from the air.

The Manor Restaurant in Motueka is without doubt the most elegant in the Nelson Province and probably one of the most elegant in the country.

The restaurant is the realisation of a 17-year dream by Lorraine Hughes who has been involved in the hospitality industry for all of her working life. It was made possible by the help and support of her engineer husband Donald who co-ordinated the restoration and setting up of the restaurant.

The restaurant is set in an old mansion in an acre and a half of ground with a mature stand of oaks, copper beech, kowhais, cabbage trees and exotics such as Oregon and sequoia pines amongst large beds of flowers.

The restaurant caters for luncheons, either in the lovely outdoor tea garden or in the main restaurant. Dinners feature an extensive menu with an emphasis on game, ultra fresh seafood, vegetables and herbs which are picked daily from a herb garden almost on the doorstep.

The decor is traditional English with an emphasis on sophistication and elegance, but the restaurant is regarded by many as having the most relaxed atmosphere—something Lorraine insists on. The staff make everyone welcome and there is nightly entertainment to make dining happy and relaxing.

It is a dining-out spot of sophistication and charm at a reasonable cost.

Facing page: Bottom, Lorraine, Donald and staff at the restaurant.

Above, the elegant main dining room.

Mid left, wine, dine and dance—the Manor has a varied programme to suit all tastes.

Bottom left, the tea garden.

It is impossible to go to Nelson without being overwhelmed by two things: the weather and the apple and pear orchards.

The drive from Nelson to Motueka along the coastal highway is an impression of a never-ending orchard running along gently sloping hills to the edge of an estuary.

The success of the orchards is due as much to the tenacity of the farmers as it is to the perfect climate for pip fruit. But the efforts of the growers and the bounty of the soil and climate would come to nothing if the rich harvest could not be shipped to the distant markets of the world and this is the job of the New Zealand Apple and Pear Marketing Board.

The Board's association with Nelson dates back to the opening of the regional office in 1953 when the Board handled 1,253,000 cartons of fruit, of which 880,000 cartons were exported and the balance sold on the New Zealand market.

Fifty per cent of the fruit was despatched from the Port of Nelson in five ships bound for the export marketplace. Another 1,000 to 5,000 cartons were shipped to Wellington on the small coastal traders that plied the coast in those days. The fruit was then reloaded in Wellington onto foreign bound vessels. The balance of the crop received was distributed on the domestic market.

Top, father and son and their crop: Brian and Rex Limmer at their Tasman orchard.

Above, heavily-laden trees at Mapua.

Facing page: Top, a bin of freshly-picked Gala apples.
Right, full bins waiting their turn at the cannery.

Today, Nelson's 203 growers contribute approximately 35 per cent of the total New Zealand crop of apples and pears handled by the Board. It is estimated this year that the Board will receive from Nelson 4,500,000 cartons of fruit. Of this total, 2,500,000 cartons will be exported while the remainder will be either distributed on the domestic market or processed by the Board's cannery at Stoke. The total Nelson export crop is now forwarded direct from the Port of Nelson.

From modest beginnings in 1953, the Board's Nelson operation is now comprehensive, reflecting the importance of the pip-fruit industry to the Nelson region. The regional office employs a staff of 36 permanents and the cannery

accounts for another 70 permanents. During the season, the regional staff increases to 140 and the cannery to 130.

Nelson is considered the home of the Board's processing operation. The cannery was completed in late January 1962 and production commenced on 12 February, 1962. Initially the output was mainly in processed apple slices. This was soon followed by apple pie filling, apple sauce and the first three lines of "Fresh-Up" apple juice. 1984 will bring a major expansion to the cannery with the installation of a $3,500,000 tetra-pak plant. This will mean that Nelson will now produce both brands of juice—"Fresh-Up" and "Just Juice". These will be packed in 250 ml and 1 litre tetra cartons.

Top left, the co-operative packhouse at Stoke.

Top right, apples being washed prior to processing at the cannery.

Mid right, some of the equipment at the cannery.

Right, cans being filled with apple juice.

Above, Springtime at Neudorf.

The visitor to the Motueka-Riwaka area during the summer holidays is immediately struck by the large area of land under tobacco cultivation—something unique to this part of New Zealand as tobacco is not grown anywhere else in the country.

Tobacco was first grown in New Zealand in 1839. It was not until the 1920s that it was grown commercially in Motueka. By the 1928/29 season 400 ha (1,000 acres) was under cultivation. Since then the industry has shown remarkable progress—the average grower now produces more than 2,500 kg/ha compared with 681 kg/ha produced in the 1920s.

It is an important crop to the area providing permanent employment for 200 people and 650 others in seasonal work. Leaf sales in 1983 brought in $8,000,000 to the district and it is anticipated that the increased 1984 crop will be worth approximately $10,000,000. The total domestic crop is purchased by two manufacturers, Rothmans Tobacco Company Limited and W D & H O Wills (NZ) Limited.

The tobacco industry provides the Government with revenue of approximately $248 million each year, based on excise duty, sales tax and other taxes.

It is an important industry in the Motueka-Riwaka area and is likely to remain so for many years to come.

Facing page: Top, the horticultural expertise required of the grower is clearly demonstrated in this familiar scene of a tobacco unit with Tasman Bay in the background.

Mid right, grower Tony Fry—removing flowers from his developed crop.

Bottom right, from the field, leaf is transported and loaded into the curing barn.

Top left, tobacco harvesting—lower leaves being picked first.

Left, cured leaf being sorted for sale.

Above, cured leaf being processed in a manufacturing company's plant in Motueka.

Mount Arthur.
Above, the track leading to the summit.
Left, the beech forest.

Facing page: Top left, Mount Arthur.
Top right, guess who?
Bottom, a mountain stream.

Facing page: Tony releasing a large brown trout.

This page: If you can recognise these scenes you will know where the river is.

The Nelson province is rightly renowned as one of the world's best trout fishing areas with trophy trout available to the skilled angler.

Tony Busch who runs Sportsgoods in Nelson is recognised as one of the best trout fishermen in the country and particularly as a man of great knowledge of trout streams and lakes in the South Island.

Tony can sometimes be persuaded to act as a fishing guide and will take the lucky anglers to his own El Dorado (see photos) a river he is not prepared to divulge.

Others can benefit from his tremendous knowledge and experience by calling at his store to purchase the literature he has published about fishing in Nelson and the South Island.

Tony was raised on the rugged West Coast in the small township of Ross. Fishing and shooting were his absorbing interests for as long as he can remember.

He joined the Police Force soon after leaving school and during his 14 years of service spent a great deal of time in sole charge of country stations in Otago and Southland, spending his off duty hours in pursuit of trout.

He is a dedicated conservationist and a fanatical catch and release advocate.

This is one of the most renowned beaches in New Zealand both for its own beauty and also as a gateway to the magnificent bays and beaches of the Abel Tasman National Park.

Kaiteriteri is a favourite with the people of Nelson as it is only an hour's drive along the spectacular coastal highway, but it is equally popular during holiday periods with people from Christchurch, Dunedin and Southland who crowd the motorcamp and the beach along with the local people.

The focus of most of the activity at the beach is the motorcamp which features first-class amenities and facilities and a little bit more as well. There is a children's playground, boat hire service, daily launch trips to the National Park and caravans which may be hired year round.

The administrators of the motorcamp claim that they have the best amenities block for paraplegics in New Zealand featuring shower, bath and toilet facilities.

Kaiteriteri's biggest attraction is its superb golden sand beach which offers safe swimming and boating in a magnificent setting. The colour of the sand if peculiar to the area confined between Kaiteriteri and Wainui Bay. It is the result of erosion of Takaka's Marble mountain which releases iron-stained quartz sand.

There is a boat ramp, store and butcher three times a week during the height of the season.

The beach is conveniently close to Motueka.

Facing page: The magnificent beach looking towards Kaka Point.

Top left, the beach from Kaka Point with the boat ramp and the motorcamp clearly visible.

Mid left, tent sites at the camp.

Bottom left, caravans at the camp.

Above, a view of the motorcamp and bay from the air.

Facing page: Top, an aerial view of Totaranui Beach and motorcamp.
Bottom, an aerial view of part of Awaroa.

Above, an aerial view of Torrent Bay with the favoured yacht and boat anchorage in the upper left.
Right, from the anchorage towards the entrance to the bay.

Previous pages: One of New Zealand's outstanding views—from Takaka Hill looking back towards Riwaka and Tasman Bay with kiwifruit, tobacco, apple and pear orchards and hop gardens in the Riwaka Valley.

Facing page : Top left, the Cobb Reservoir.
Bottom left, an aerial view of part of Golden Bay showing some of Pohara Beach and the township of Takaka in the upper left.
Top right, the main street of Takaka.
Mid right, the famous Rat Trap.
Bottom right, exposed marble rock on Takaka Hill.

Top, a view of Collingwood.
Above, a view on the way to Collingwood.

Facing page: Top left, a view from the Grove.

Bottom left, a view inside the Grove.

Top right, Upper Takaka Valley from the main road.

Bottom right, Takaka's famous tame eels being fed with blancmange.

This page, some houses in Golden Bay.

Much of the economic lifeblood of Takaka and the surrounding district depends on the Golden Bay Dairy Co-operative Company.

This company is one of the largest employers in the district as well as the processing backbone of the 150 suppliers who farm dairy cows in the area.

The company was formed and commenced business near its present site just outside town in 1901. In that year the company manufactured about 30 tonnes of butter as compared with the 2,352 tonnes it manufactures each year now.

During the intervening years between its establishment and the present, the company has amalgamated and generally expanded its facilities to become the sole milk processor in the Golden Bay area.

The company services an area of more than 500 square kilometres giving its tanker drivers some 179,000 kilometres to travel during the course of the season. On the average each year the tankers collect 54.5 million litres of whole milk of which 2,518,790 kg is milk fat. The high quality of the product was shown in the fact that 98.4% of the wholemilk collected from suppliers graded finest under the standard plate count and senses test.

As well as manufacturing butter for the local and export markets, the company produces casein and buttermilk powders also for export.

The company employs some 60 staff, owns 13 staff houses, has an interest in a subsidiary distribution company which distributes butter, cheese, eggs, yoghurt and other products to the retail trade.

Top, the outside view.
Mid right, staff pose in the casein.
Right, butter extruded.

The Whole Meal Trading Company of Takaka began its life as a cafe and health food shop and has developed into a restaurant and art gallery, initially for local artists and now also for artists outside the valley and some displays of an international flavour, such as a recent exhibition of Japanese wood block prints.

The restaurant and shop are run by a happy partnership of Peter Bridges and Judith Ansell. Both believe in serving wholesome, healthy food with an emphasis on a wide range of salads, a fact I can vouch for. I enjoyed one of the nicest salads in my life in their restaurant. The restaurant also serves a wide range of popular dishes such as omelettes, veal, beef and fish.

One of the most popular dishes, however, is salmon from Takaka's own Bubbling Springs Salmon Farm. It is served after being baked in the oven in wine and herbs and orange juice.

Top, Peter and Judith at the counter with the menu behind them.

Mid left, a view of the restaurant and gallery.

Bottom left, a range of health foods.

151

Much of Nelson's outdoors can now be enjoyed in a less rugged way than the usual Kiwi style with boots and pack. Back Trax Tours offer comfortable four-wheel drive safaris to Golden Bay, the Nelson Lakes, and Molesworth Station, and whitewater rafting on the Gowan and Buller rivers.

Rafting with Back Trax is a whole day affair, leaving Nelson early in the morning, arriving at Lake Rotoroa in time for morning tea and then rafting down the Gowan from where it empties from the lake to its confluence with the Buller. Here the rafts pull ashore for a well-earned lunch and then continue down the river through some mighty rapids. The day ends at Nelson at about 5.30 pm.

For those who crave a view of New Zealand's true back-country the Back Trax two-day safari through part of the historical Molesworth Station is recommended.

Facing page: canoes on the Pelorus River.

Above, through the Granity rapids on the Buller.
Left, Down the Gowan River.

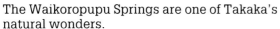

The Waikoropupu Springs are one of Takaka's natural wonders.

A vast volume of water, averaging some 14 cubic metres per second (3,080 gallons per second), gushes from the ground. It is interesting to note that the average age of the water appearing at the springs is between three and four years old. During its time in the ground, before it wells up to the surface, this water goes through many purifying processes as it works its way through Takaka's 500-million-year-old marble.

On the true left side of the springs and some short distance from their origin is the Bubbling Springs Salmon Farm.

The farm was established in 1977 and since that time has expanded to provide employment to four people as well as adding capacity to a local processing plant.

There are 11 concrete raceways where the fish are raised from ova to table and smoker size. This year the total capacity produced was 50 tonnes, of which 20 tonnes were of large premium quality for smoking.

During the time the farm has been in operation thousands of salmon have been released to follow their normal life cycle of going down the river to the sea and then returning at maturity.

The farm intends to keep releasing numbers of such fish in the hope of building up a large run in years to come. Visitors are welcome by arrangement but unfortunately regulations precludes gate sales.

Facing page: Top left, the main spring at the Waikoropupu Springs.

Top right, entering the cave which is the source of the Riwaka River. (*D M Boulton*).

Left, inside the cave. Source of the Riwaka River. (*D M Boulton*).

Right, a diver amongst the dancing sands. (*D M Boulton*).

Top, a view of the farm.

Mid left, harvested fish being netted for processing.

Left, an underwater view in one of the ponds. (*D M Boulton*).

The Hitching Post restaurant is named after an old Nelson landmark, the original hitching posts which still stand, but which now form the supports of the verandah of the restaurant.

It is a family business run by Michael and Margaret Bennett who work hard at fostering a congenial, relaxed atmosphere for their clients.

The Hitching Post consists of two parts: the main indoor restaurant/cafe and an attractive open courtyard at the back of the premises which is pleasant in summer and during the winter because of Nelson's warm sunny days. The courtyard is fringed with grape and kiwifruit vines and these bear prolifically. The bright red of bougainvillae contrasts with the white of the tables and chairs.

A feature of the courtyard is the outdoor barbeque set where Michael will cook steak or fish to your liking.

Michael is also renowned for his pizzas and the visitor may sometimes see him tossing the pastry as a demonstration of how it should be done to achieve just the right texture.

In the cool of the winter evenings the restaurant is cosy with a pot belly stove and visitors are made to feel welcome for as long as they wish to stay.

Top, the courtyard at lunchtime.
Right, Michael showing his expertise by tossing the pizza dough.

Top, a view of Tasman Bay with Fifeshire Rock dominant.   Above, a view of Nelson hillside homes.

Above, Lake Rotoiti (*Peter Braggins*).

Top right, yacht regatta Lake Rotoiti (*John Acheson*).

Right, Travers Falls (*Peter Braggins*).

Centre right, skiing at Mount Robert (*John Acheson*).

Bottom right, approaching Mount Angelus on a cross country trek (*Peter Braggins*).

Facing page: Top, climbing Mount Cupola with Mount Hopeless in the background (*Peter Braggins*).

Mid right, tramping party camp on the Spenser Mountains (*Photo John Acheson*).

Bottom, school party descending Mount Robert above Lake Rotoiti (*John Acheson*).

Facing page: Top left, one of the bushwalks adjacent to the Lodge.
Top right, the stream on the way to the waterfall.
Bottom, a view of Lake Rotoroa from the Lodge.

Above, rata blooming on the side of Lake Rotoroa. Mount Misery beyond.

Lake Rotoroa in the Nelson Lakes National Park is one of the gems of the Nelson Province and Lake Rotoroa is without doubt one of the most attractive hostelries in New Zealand.

It is not just its magnificent setting with the bush plunging down steep, snow clad mountains to the water's edge, or the lovely walks and the superb trout fishing. It is as much part of the tasteful old world charm of the lodge itself and the three partners who run it.

The lodge is an ideal destination for those who enjoy the outdoors but want a comfortable (in this case somewhat luxurious) base. The day can be spent hiking along the numerous walks, motoring to points of interest in the area, trout fishing in the lake or the nearby rivers, stalking deer or chamois, or in the winter enjoying one of two nearby ski fields.

Guests énjoy pre-dinner drinks before a blazing log fire once the weather gets cooler and then are called to the grand dining salon.

The lodge prides itself on its cuisine and the personal attention of the management.

Facing page: Top, The Lodge.
Bottom, mine hosts, Robert Haswell, and Collette and Alastair Benfield.

Top left, from the entrance hall looking towards the dining room.
Upper left, one of the bedrooms.
Lower left, a sterling silver dinnerset on display.
Bottom left, the stately dining room during the course of dinner.

The new luxury lodge at Lake Rotoiti will put the magnificent Nelson Lakes National Park region on the international tourist map. Boasting twenty fully-serviced double rooms, Alpine Lodge Rotoiti is located in the heart of St Arnaud village on the shores of the lake. An hour's drive from Nelson or Blenheim, the Lodge also has direct air access twenty minutes from Wellington at the Speargrass airstrip (eight minutes from Alpine Lodge).

Operating under a Tourist House Licence, the Lodge provides the only hotel accommodation in the area.

The two accommodation wings are respectively named Robert and Rainbow after the nearby ski fields. A stay at the Lodge offers unparalleled opportunities in winter and summer for a wide range of tourist activities including skiing, fishing, boating, tramping, hunting and just relaxing.

To commemorate the discoverer of Lake Rotoiti the owners of the Lodge have named its spacious restaurant the J S Cotterell room. In addition to the fully licenced restaurant with seating capacity for 100, the Lodge offers conference and seminar facilities in the Travers Room named after the nearby river.

Tastefully designed by leading Nelson architect, Ian Jack, the Lodge should live up to the prediction made more than a century ago by Julius von Haast: "I had no idea that such a jewel in point of landscape existed so near Nelson and I am sure that the time is not far distant when this spot will become the favourite abode of those whose means and leisure will permit them to admire picturesque scenery."

Facing page: Top, Lake Rotoiti from Mount Robert.
Bottom, the Alpine Lodge.

Mid left, an example of one of the bedrooms which features a loft with additional space for two.
Bottom left, the Lodge Restaurant.

Without doubt, one of the most interesting places to visit in the Nelson-Golden Bay area is Farewell Spit. This can only be done by joining the Collingwood Safari Tour which is authorised to take visitors to the end of the spit where the lighthouse is sited.

It is essential to make bookings for the tours both to be sure to get on and to find out when the safari leaves Collingwood as this is very much dependent on the tide.

Because the spit is a nature reserve access is restricted to the safari tours except for fishermen who may use a small section of the outer beach and those who want to walk for a distance of 2½ kilometres on the inner beach.

The reason for such extreme caution is due to the spit's significance as New Zealand's most important wading bird habitat and this is confirmed by the fact that it is only one of two areas in New Zealand designated as a wetland of international importance.

The spit is 35 kilometres long and up to 6.5 kilometres wide at low water. It is composed of sand driven north from the West Coast, deposited along the spit or brought into Golden Bay where it is imperceptibly filling in the bay.

Farewell Spit's most important residents are some 90 species of birds. Amongst these the most prolific are the waders. These include the bar-tailed godwit of which there are between 12,000

and 19,000, and the knot which number between 16,000 and 27,000. Among the others are the Mongolian dotterel, the wrybill, the long-billed curlew, the little whimbrel, the grey-tailed tattler, the turnstone as well as wekas which will greet you at the light and common introduced birds.

The fascinating history of these wading birds reveals their amazing life-cycle: each spring they arrive in New Zealand from the tundra of Siberia where they spent their summer breeding. The 12,000 kilometre journey is repeated again in the autumn when the birds marshall into huge flocks at the spit and eventually leave to return to Siberia in one of the most amazing migrations known.

An ideal way to explore much of Golden Bay is to stay at the Tukurua Motor Camp only a short distance from Collingwood.

The camp is sighted next to a magnificent beach with safe swimming and well clear of the main road so that there is no anxiety for the safety of children.

The camp offers 200 sites and 60 of these are connected with power. There are six cabins, two kitchen blocks, clean showers and toilets and a well stocked camp store.

The camp is probably the most central in the bay for the various attractions which include tramping, as well as the famous Heaphy track, fishing for trout and sea fish, Farewell Spit, Pupu

Springs, early goldfields, the famous tame eels, rare snails and limestone caves.

Facing Page: Left, the safari trucks.
Top, giant sand dunes on the way to the lighthouse.
Lower right, the lighthouse.

Above left, climbing and sliding.
Above, the last keeper before the light becomes automatic.
Top right, the friendly wekas.
Mid right, the friendly tourists.
Lower right, Tukurua Motorcamp has a lovely beach.
Bottom right, it is an ideal family camping ground.

Top, an aerial view showing the Wainui Inlet which borders the north-western extremity of the park.

Above, Marahau at the start of the Abel Tasman National Park from the Tasman Bay end, is popular with holidaymakers.

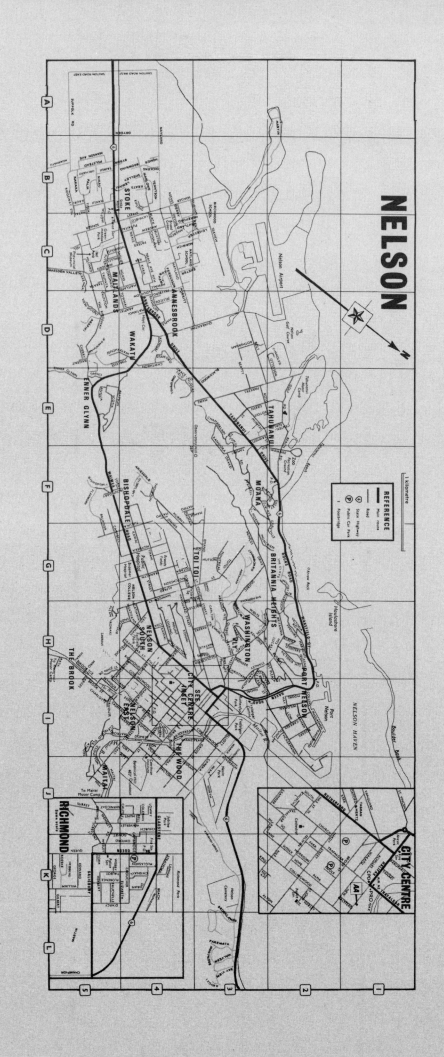

NELSON